Plants For Play

Other books from **MIG**Communications for your play design library:

Play For All Guidelines
Planning, Design, and Management of Outdoor Play Settings
for All Children
Robin C. Moore, Susan M. Goltsman, Daniel S. Iacofano, editors

Childhood's Domain
Play and Place in Child Development
Robin C. Moore

Safety First
Inspection and Maintenance Program for Play Areas
Sally McIntyre and Susan M. Goltsman

Natural Learning
The Life History of an Environmental Schoolyard
Robin C. Moore and Herb H. Wong

Plants For Play

A Plant Selection Guide for Children's Outdoor Environments

Robin C. Moore

Communications

Berkeley, California

MIG Communications, 800 Hearst Avenue, Berkeley, CA 94710, USA
(510) 845-7549; fax (510) 845-8750

Second printing 2002

Managing Editor: David Driskell
Graphic Design: Anne Endrusick, Tim Lehane
Production Assistant: Christopher Hamilton
Copyeditor: Mi Yung Rhee

Library of Congress Cataloging-in-Publication Data
Moore, Robin C.
    Plants for play: a plant selection guide for children's outdoor
environments / Robin C. Moore.
        p. cm.
    Includes bibliographical references (p.) and indexes.
    ISBN 0-944661-18-1
    1. Plants for play environments.   I. Title.
SB457.2.M66   1993
712'.5'093—dc20   92-62234

 Printed on recycled paper

To The Reader: The authors, editors, publishers, contributors, and others involved in
the preparation of this document assume no risk or liability for incidents arising from
the application of this information in any way whatsoever.

How To Use This Book

This book is for anyone who is trying to make informed decisions about what plants to include in an outdoor play environment, be it a large public play area or a backyard. It will help you understand the importance of plants in play settings and assist you in the selection of plants that serve different functions and support child development.

Begin using the book by reviewing the table of contents. It will give you an overview of the range of functions that plants can serve in play settings. Read the book's introductory chapter to become familiar with the many ways in which plants can add value to any outdoor space used by children. Then start flipping back and forth through the plant lists and narrative introductions in the main body of the book to learn how specific plants can support children's play experiences.

To apply the contents of this book, you will first need to consider the functional aspects of your site. Identify locations that have good access to the sun, areas that need to be screened from the wind, and places where erosion might be a problem. Determine the constraints posed by soil type and drainage conditions. The introductory narratives to the tables on *Shade Quality*, *Screens*, *Erosion Control*, and *Drought Tolerance* provide information that may be of use in this regard. You will also need to identify the plant hardiness zone in which you are located (see the map on pages 84 and 85).

You must also consider the play opportunities you wish to provide and where such opportunities might be located on your site. Identify locations that lend themselves to climbing, swinging, hiding, interaction with "play props," harvesting of fruits and nuts, or exploration of different textures and fragrances. Determine how much emphasis you would like to place on these activities that children enjoy so much, and how they should be distributed throughout the site.

You may also want to consider selecting plants that attract wildlife. Children love to hunt for insects, butterflies, and small mammals, and many young people enjoy observing birds. You can provide for these activities throughout the site or concentrate some of them in particular areas.

Other functional or aesthetic principles must also be considered. Issues of design style, for instance. A naturalistic style will emphasize indigenous species while a more formal style will incorporate elements such as avenues or grid-patterned orchards. You will also want to include other landscape elements besides plants: rocks, water features, play structures, seating areas, grade changes, etc.

As you consider the many variables affecting your planting design, particular species will begin to emerge as the favored choices. This book will help you make choices that are sensitive to the important role that plants serve in the play experiences of children. Depending on your knowledge of individual species, additional publications and/or a landscape architect may also need to be consulted.

Eventually, design issues will be resolved and a planting design will emerge and be installed. Over the years, the plants in your play area will grow and mature. Some will do very well, while others may do poorly and require replacement. Nonetheless, with a little thought and proper planning, these plants will provide a wide range of activities for children to explore and enjoy.

A key role in the initial stages of the creation of this book was played by Julia Barringer who worked closely with me to develop the bulk of the plant selections in each of the main categories. These were later checked for accuracy by Susan Gular.

Special thanks are due to landscape architect Susan Little and horticulturalist Sarah Price for carefully and expertly reviewing the final version of the manuscript.

I am especially grateful for David Driskell's many editorial suggestions that have considerably improved the clarity and usability of the book. David, graphic designers Anne Endrusick and Tim Lehane, production assistant Christopher Hamilton, and other members of the MIG Communications team gave much care and attention to the production of the book, always striving for the highest level of quality.

The idea for the book would never have happened without the input and enthusiasm of the scores of children I have worked with over the years who have demonstrated so clearly and dramatically that vegetation serves a unique and essential role in their play spaces. Time and time again, in inner city, suburban, and county locations, these children have given me fresh insights by allowing me to observe their behavior, by talking with me about their activities, and by expressing their appreciation of and feelings toward their natural play environments. To them, this book is dedicated.

Robin C. Moore was born in London, England. He holds degrees in architecture (London University) and urban and regional planning (MIT) and works as a designer and design researcher in urban planning, architecture, landscape architecture, and interior, product, and graphic design. He has a longstanding research interest in the relationship between child development and natural environments in cities.

During the 1970s, Mr. Moore was a member of an interdisciplinary community participation team that developed the Environmental Yard, a community recreational and educational garden in Berkeley, California. He was a cofounder of Play and Learning in Adaptable Environments (PLAE), a program to integrate children with disabilities into the community through environmental and recreational programming.

Mr. Moore is a professor of Landscape Architecture at the School of Design, North Carolina State University (NCSU), and former chair of the Environmental Design Research Association (EDRA). He is the author of *Childhood's Domain: Play and Place in Child Development* (MIG Communications, 1986) and many articles about children's environments. He is coauthor of the *Play For All Guidelines* (MIG Communications, 1987) and *Natural Learning: The Life History of an Environmental Schoolyard* (MIG Communications 1997).

Mr. Moore is a principal of Moore Iacofano Goltsman. His most recent work has focused on children and family play environments in the United States and Latin America. He is currently President of the International Association for the Child's Right to Play (IPA) and editor of the IPA magazine, *PlayRights*.

Chapter One

Introduction

Plants for Play

Over the years, I have conducted many design programming workshops with adults who work with children. As a warm-up exercise, I often ask the participants to think about the places from their childhood that they remember most vividly and to jot down some notes about the physical elements that made the places so memorable. I have conducted this exercise in many parts of the world, in many cultures; yet, regardless of the circumstances, elements of the natural environment (water, vegetation, animals, soil, rocks, sunlight) are nearly always the first thing people recall. Of these elements, plants in one form or another are the most frequently mentioned.

This book is primarily directed to those who feel that plants (trees, shrubs, flowers, vegetables, etc.) are an essential part of children's environments. I hope the book will be a useful source of guidance in the design and management of children's landscapes as well as an effective tool for convincing others that plants are an invaluable resource for play and child development.

Plants As Play Settings
Plants can be designed into many different types of play settings, but they should also be considered as play settings in and of themselves. Individually, collectively, or in combination with people-made elements, different types of plants can greatly extend the range of play activity: collecting plant parts, climbing and playing in trees, hide-and-seek games, and general exploration. Together with soil, sand, and water, plants provide manipulative settings that are quite different from the static, unchangeable character of fixed play structures.

"The flowers are magic," a girl says very matter-of-factly, "especially these." She bends down and picks some scarlet flax. "They'll make your hands magic, then everything you touch'll be magic. Pens will write magic, glasses will see magic. Everything'll be magic." [1]

Because of their interactive properties, plants provide intrinsically interesting, open-ended settings that stimulate exploration and discovery, dramatic play, and imagination. In the Environmental Yard (a highly diversified, action-research play and learning space developed on the grounds of a California elementary school), detailed observational studies conducted over several years demonstrated that, when provided, children use vegetation as a basic resource for playing and learning.

Plants stimulate all of the senses—touch, sight, taste, smell, and hearing—so it is not surprising that children are closely tuned to vegetated environments. Plants also encourage a peaceful outlook on life and add a positive ambiance to play settings through their mix of sun, shade, color, texture, fragrance, and softness of enclosure.

Some General Guidelines

The following guidelines should be considered for all plantings in children's outdoor environments:

- Vary the texture of leaves: evergreen with deciduous; shiny with rough; serrated with smooth edges; thin with thick.
- Vary the form, size, and shape of plants.
- Select plants that emphasize seasonal change: evergreen contrasted with deciduous; seasonal color; early leaves; late flowers; seeds, nuts, and fruit.
- Consider opportunities for color in trees, ground covers, vines, annuals, and perennials.
- Select plants for fragrance.
- Select plants for craft and culinary activities.

- Select plants for auditory stimulation. Some plants, especially in the fall, produce interesting sounds when the wind blows through their dry leaves. Plants like bamboo and pine trees produce sounds year-round.

Plants As Design Elements

Plants can serve a variety of purposes in the design of children's outdoor environments:

Enclosure. The size, shape, and enclosure of play spaces can be enhanced by being wholly or partially defined with plants. This is because plants provide more boundary depth than plain fencing, thereby extending spatial variety. The highly varied spatial and textural qualities of plants increase the range of possible behaviors and add to the complexity and subtlety of games and social interactions. Plant-enclosed spaces make ideal settings for chase and hide-and-go-seek games and mature shrubs make excellent hideouts and refuges.[2] Plants also help soften the transition between indoors and outdoors—especially for people who have difficulty adjusting to sudden changes in light levels.

Identity. Distinctive plantings and specimen plants provide visual identity and a sense of place to children's environments. This helps children and the general community retain strong positive memories of their experiences. People of all ages respond to flowering shrubs, deciduous trees, rockeries, banked borders of flowers, herb gardens, and the imaginative forms of public garden design. If the overall design is pleasing and attractive, residents will see the play area as a valuable addition to their community.

"It makes you feel like you're in a special place. You can hide around in the bushes and spy on people or play hide-and-go-seek, which at any regular school you can't do. It's just neat."[3]

Movement. The experience of movement through play areas can be greatly enhanced by using plants in relation to topography. As in the classic "circuit" or strolling gardens found in many cultures, plants can be used along paths to create a sequence of views, textures, smells, light, shade, and color. For children's environments, gardens should be designed for running and chasing as well as for strolling (which children will also do if the vegetation is interesting and intimately laid out). Specimen trees can be used as orienting elements.

Climbing. Tree-climbing is universally popular. Some species of trees and shrubs provide excellent support for climbing and swinging. The problem is that in many potential play spaces—from private residential yards to public parks and gardens—plants are viewed as hands-off aesthetic enhancements provided solely for adult enjoyment. When children use plants for *their* purposes, child-adult conflicts often result. For this reason, consider planting (or conserving) some trees or tree-like shrubs that can be designated for climbing—with an adequate shock-absorbing surface such as wood chips installed underneath.[4]

Play Props. Vegetation supplies a wide variety of play resources that children can harvest for themselves.[5] There is no substitute for plant-generated play props. Leaves, flowers, fruits, nuts, seeds, and sticks stimulate an infinite variety of imaginative responses.

Programmed Activities/Education. Plants can be used to support many different program activities that require spatial diversity and a stimulating atmosphere.[6] Trees and shrubs are good for building in and provide branches from which play items and structures can be suspended. Plant settings are essential for environmental education programs, especially on school grounds.[8] Plants provide a variety of learning materials that are virtually free of cost. For example, many annuals and perennials are suitable for craft activities such as dying and doll-making.

Accessibility/Integration. Plant settings can create intimate, touchable spaces that are accessible to children with disabilities and therefore offer particular advantages as integrated settings. A mix of natural and people-made elements will attract children of all abilities, providing excellent opportunities for child-to-child interaction and shared experiences that integrate children naturally.[9] For this reason alone, every effort should be made to integrate plants into all outdoor play settings, especially in manufactured equipment areas, rather than restricting plants to segregated "nature areas."

Landmarks. Objects with a clear visual identity, such as trees, large rocks, and aquatic features, function as landmarks. They give the user a memorable sense of place and a feeling of security.

Seasonal Change. Plants mark the passing of seasons and introduce children to a sense of time and natural processes. A diverse mix of plant types can provide never-ending sequences of change, sensory stimulation, and educational opportunities.

Wildlife Enhancement. It is important for children to interact with wildlife as an environmental education resource.[10] Plants support wildlife by providing essential food and shelter. Plants that bear fruits, cones, and seeds attract birds, squirrels, butterflies, and insect populations, all of which fascinate children and stimulate their imaginations. Children can get actively involved by constructing habitats such as bird-

"I make little horses out of pieces of wood and sit under the willow tree by the stream with one of my friends. It feels good there. Really quiet. Lots of kids just like to sit there and talk." [11]

houses. Indigenous plant communities provide a range of habitat conditions to support a variety of animal communities. These habitats should not be overly manicured or "tidied-up." This removes many of the loose materials that animals depend on for survival.[12]

Climate Modification. Because plants are so varied, they provide a greater range of microclimatic choice than people-made structures. Adults and children both dislike being hot, but children heat up more quickly than adults because of their smaller mass. For young children in hot climates, shade is extremely important. Natural shade in play spaces encourages day-long summertime use. Shade is particularly important for metal play equipment that can become hazardous when exposed to hot sun. Trees are the best way to provide shade, particularly spreading, deciduous species that shed their leaves to let in winter sun. Trees and shrubs can also provide excellent shelter from the wind.

Environmental Quality. Plants in play areas are an important determinant of environmental quality. Erosion, for instance, is a common problem in children's play areas. This is because space for play is often relegated to marginal land that is difficult to build on due to steep topography or poor drainage. On heavily used sites, regardless of the quality of the land, erosion can become a problem unless appropriate remedial action is taken. Effective management of surface water runoff emphasizes percolation of water back into the ground to replenish local aquifers. To this end, broad-leaved deciduous trees can be effective in reducing the direct impact of heavy rain on exposed ground surfaces, thereby extending the runoff time and allowing more time for the water to soak back into the soil. Plants with shallow, lateral root systems may help bind the soil to resist erosion from young feet as well as rain.

"It's the only place in the whole world like this, with pretty ponds and trees and birds that come out. It's just a good-natured place. It gives me a new idea every day. It makes me feel like I can make skyscrapers and buildings out of sticks and sand. It's not too hot either, it's cool but not cold. The trees make shade. Kids learn about birds and trees and fish. And maybe they learn they can't push other people around." [13]

Use of Native and Introduced Species. Interest in the use of native vegetation in landscape design has been growing for many years. The most important reason to consider native species for play areas is that they are key components of the ecological and cultural heritage of the local region, and offer children highly significant experiential learning opportunities. Another reason often given for using native vegetation is survival. In many cases, native plants will be hardier and less likely to incur disease or insect problems because they are suited to the physical conditions of the region. However, this is not necessarily the case in the harsh, desertlike conditions of the urban environment. In these conditions, introduced species may actually perform better than native species.

When designing with native species, it is important to think of them as associated communities of plants—along with the animals that find food and shelter there. The design objective should be to replicate the conditions of the natural habitat of these communities as closely as possible in the play space (in terms of aspect, soils, drainage, etc.).

In outdoor settings for children, a mix of species is often the preferred approach. With careful design, native plantings can provide a foundation of small meadows, thickets, brushlands, and woodlands for free play, exploration, and learning activities. Exotic or introduced species can be used selectively to give a special identity to the play setting, to increase the diversity of play props, to enhance sensory variety, and to increase the resiliency of the plant setting as a whole. Cultivars of either native or introduced species can be used to provide bigger flowers, better foliage, more intense color, or varied forms.

Drought Resistance. The increasing interest in native vegetation and the use of drought-tolerant species provide further direction to the planting design choices for children's outdoor spaces. Interaction with these plant communities can have an important educational impact on children, giving them the knowledge necessary to make conservation-based decisions as adults.

Planning and Managing Plants for Play

Plants add a critical dimension of change and diversity to children's environments. They greatly extend the range of sensory stimulation beyond that which can be provided by synthetic, manufactured objects. Ever-changing, instantly responding to variations in the weather, expressing seasonal cycles, presenting fluctuating palettes of texture, color, form, fragrance, and sound, plants are unmatched in their ability to stimulate the senses and create a positive aesthetic effect.

Plants in children's play areas need to be carefully managed. If vegetated settings are to be child-relevant, they will never be maintenance-free. To ensure proper attention to plants, the importance of vegetation as a childhood resource must be recognized in public policy. Expert vegetation management must be provided in areas used by children, with pruning regimes and other maintenance procedures that respond to play and learning requirements.

As a first step, a list of local plants should be developed—using this book as a guide—to identify the most appropriate regional species for purposes such as play value, wildlife habitat, and shade quality. Local species that are highly poisonous or otherwise unsuitable in children's play environments should also be highlighted. These lists can then be used to evaluate existing plantings in children's outdoor spaces, to select additional species, and to develop new designs that will provide a complete palette of plants to support children's play experiences.

A Note on Omissions

There are two topics which have been purposely omitted from this book. The first is the broad topic of wetlands and aquatic plants. While wetland and aquatic environments provide extremely valuable play and learning opportunities for children, the possibilities for developing such environments as children's play settings is extremely difficult, particularly in the United States, due to complex liability and maintenance issues. Such issues can only be addressed with specific, practical design solutions. Listings of aquatic plants by themselves, not tied to design, would not be meaningful or useful. Readers interested in aquatic design should consult Graham Flatt's *Pond Design Guide for Schools*.[14]

The second omission is the topic of gardening. Although flower and vegetable gardening activities are very important to children, the topic has already been addressed in great detail elsewhere. Numerous resource materials and guidebooks are available that address children's gardening specifically and community gardening in general. They should be consulted for listings of garden vegetables and flowers. Another useful reference is the *Play For All Guidelines*.[15] It provides design information on children's gardens as well as an overview of design issues related to children's aquatic environments.

Endnotes

1. Robin C. Moore, "Plants as Play Props," *Children's Environments Quarterly* 6(1) (1989): 3-6.

2. Mary Ann Kirkby, "Nature as Refuge," Children and Vegetation, a special issue of *Children's Environments Quarterly* 6(1) (1989):7-12.

3. Robin C. Moore, "Before and After Asphalt: Diversity as an Ecological Measure of Quality," in A. Pellegrini and M.N. Bloch, eds., *The Ecological Context of Children's Play* (Norwood, NJ: Ablex, 1989), 203.

4. Robin C. Moore, Susan M. Goltsman, and Daniel S. Iacofano, *Play For All Guidelines: Planning, Design, and Management of Outdoor Play Settings for All Children*, 2nd ed. (Berkeley, CA: MIG Communications, 1992). Refer to pp. 117-127 for comprehensive information on safety surfaces.

5. Moore, "Plants as Play Props," 3-6.

6. Linda Allison, *The Reasons for Seasons: The Great Cosmic Megagalactic Trip Without Moving From Your Chair* (Boston: Little, Brown and Company, 1975); Jacklyn Johnston, *Nature Areas for City People* (London: London Ecology Unit, Bedford House, 125 Camden High St., London NW17JR; 1990); Moore, "Plants as Play Props," 3-6; Robin C. Moore and Herbert H. Wong, *Another Way of Learning: Child Development in Natural Settings* (Berkeley, CA: MIG Communications, in press).

7. Moore, "Plants as Play Props," 3.

8. Eileen Adams, *Learning Through Landscapes: A Report on the Use, Design, Management, and Development of School Grounds* (London: Learning Through Landscape Trust, Technology House, Victoria Road, Winchester Hants, S023 7DU, U.K.; 1990); Kirsty Young, *Using School Grounds as an Educational Resource* (London: Learning Through Landscape Trust, 1990); Department of Education and Science, *The Outdoor Classroom: Educational Use, Landscape Design, and Management of School Grounds*, Building Bulletin 71, (London: Her Majesty's Stationery Office, 1990).

9. John Mason, *The Environment of Play* (West Point, NY: Leisure Press, 1982); Robin C. Moore and Linda Schneekloth, eds., Children and Vegetation, a special issue of *Children's Environments Quarterly* 6(1) (1989).

10. D.L. Leedy, "Planning for Wildlife in Cities and Suburbs," *Urban Wildlife* (Washington, DC: Superintendent of Documents, U.S. Government Printing Office, 1982); Lisa Schicker, "Children, Wildlife, and Residential Developments," (Master's thesis, North Carolina State University, School of Design, 1986).

11. Moore, "Before and After Asphalt," 201.

12. City of Seattle, *Guidelines for Play Areas: Recommendations for Planning, Design, and Maintenance* (Seattle, WA: Department of Parks and Recreation, 1986).

13. Moore, "Before and After Asphalt," 203.

14. Graham Flatt, *Pond Design Guide for Schools* (Marsh Barton, Exeter: Wheaton Publishers, 1989). See also Johnston, *Nature Areas for City People* and Department of Education and Science, *The Outdoor Classroom*.

15. Moore, Goltsman, and Iacofano, *Play For All Guidelines*.

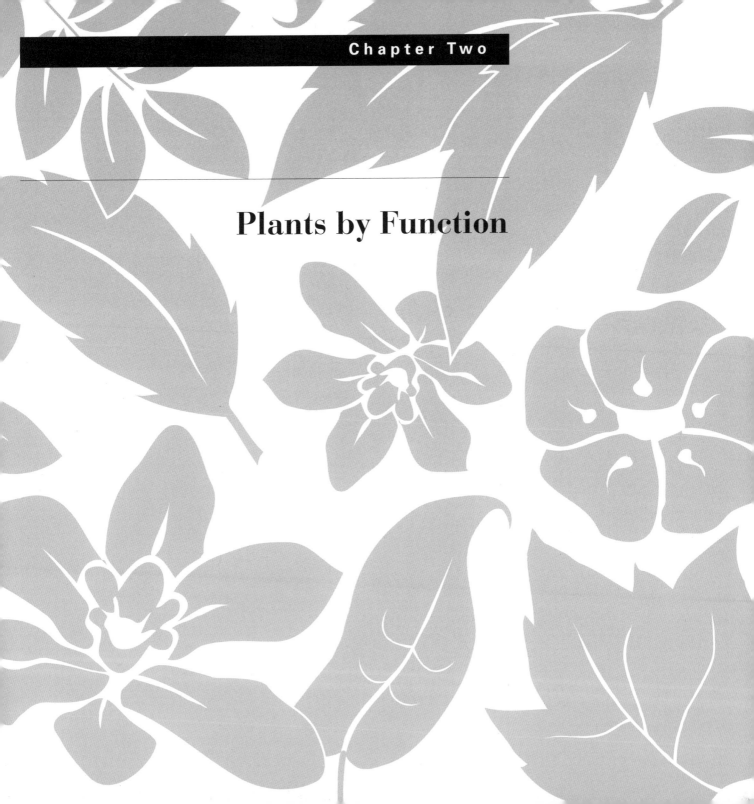

Chapter Two

Plants by Function

Overview

Following are lists of plants that serve various functions in children's outdoor play environments. The functional listings included in this chapter are:

- **Sensory Variety**
  Fragrance, Texture, Wind Effects

- **Play Value**
  Climbing & Swinging, Hiding Places, Play Props

- **Nature's Bounty**
  Fruits, Herbs & Nuts

- **Seasonal Interest**
  Fall Color, Winter Berries & Evergreens, Winter Tracery & Bark, Winter Flowers, Spring Harbingers

- **Shade Quality**

- **Screens**
  Physical Barriers, Wind Screens & Visual Buffers

- **Wildlife Enhancement**

- **Erosion Control**

- **Drought Tolerance**

Each plant list contains information that may be useful in selecting an appropriate species to meet your needs. Be sure to read the section *How to Read the Plant Lists* on page 21 before you begin using the lists.

The map on pages 84 and 85 should also be consulted to identify the "plant hardiness zone" in which you live. This will help you determine which plants are appropriate for your area (zones are identified for every plant in the plant lists). In addition, be sure to review Chapter Three, *Poisonous Plants and Pesticides* for a discussion of factors you should consider when addressing the issue of poisonous plants in children's play areas. A list of the most common poisonous plant species is also provided.

The *Index of Plant Names* in Chapter Five is useful for identifying plants that serve multiple functions. It should be consulted during the plant selection process to identify plants that meet particular sets of needs (e.g., a tree that provides both shade quality and play value or a flowering plant that is both fragrant and drought-resistant).

The intent of the lists is to give guidance. They are by no means comprehensive. As you become familiar with the ways in which plants can support children's play, you may find other plant species that better meet your local conditions and requirements. As you do so, you will begin to develop a custom list of regional favorites that do well in your area and provide a varied and stimulating environment for children.

Common Names and Botanical Names

The plants in this book are primarily organized by common name because these are the names that most people will find most familiar. However, be aware that any single plant may have several different common names associated with it. Likewise, one common name might be used to refer to several different plant species, depending on where you are geographically located.

Whenever a plant name is listed, both its common name and botanical name (or Latin name) are given to avoid any confusion between plants. The botanical name always appears in italics following the common name. It is critical that you reference the botanical name whenever purchasing plants for your play area.

Plants and Accessibility

Plants provide an excellent play medium for the integration of children of all abilities, providing an important ingredient of "universal design" to any play environment. However, no special plant list is provided here for "accessible" plants because nearly any plant can promote integration and accessibility if it is appropriately selected and located in the play environment.

To encourage positive interaction between children of different abilities, choose species that branch vertically and provide play interest between 18 to 48 inches from the ground. This will ensure optimum access for children who use wheelchairs. Containers offer an excellent means for bringing plant material to this height. Attention should also be given to the types of surfacing in the play area. Be sure to provide hard surfaced paths that allow children using wheelchairs to get up close to plants and participate in plant-oriented play.

Children with visual disabilities also enjoy plants. Vivid colors, a range of scents, and a variety of textures can provide fun and pleasure for everyone. Refer to the plant lists for *Sensory Variety* (*Fragrance, Texture,* and *Wind Effects*) and *Seasonal Interest* (*Fall Color* and *Spring Harbingers*) for plant species appropriate for children with visual disabilities. Shade is also an important feature for many children and adults with disabilities. The plant list on *Shade Quality* will help you identify appropriate species for ensuring year-round comfort for all users.

Region-Specific Species

Most of the plants listed here have been selected because of their broad hardiness characteristics. Many species are not listed because they are specific to a few regions. As a result, many species that grow in the southwest and western regions, particularly California, are underrepresented. However, a number of the most outstanding western species have been included along with references to the *Sunset Western Garden Book,* a useful guide to western plants. This and other references are listed in Chapter Six and should be consulted for additional information.

How to Read the Plant Lists

The plant lists that appear in this chapter are presented in table format. They provide information on various plant characteristics that may be important in selecting a plant species appropriate for your play area. Each plant list includes the following information:

- **Common Name.** This appears in the first column of every table. Plants are listed alphabetically by common name, with subgroupings where appropriate (e.g., Ground Covers, Coniferous Trees, etc.).

- **Botanical Name.** This is the Latin name identifying the plant genus, species, and variety, where appropriate.

- **Zone.** This identifies the "plant hardiness zones" in which each plant may be grown. The 1990 USDA map identifying zones in the U.S. is shown on pages 84 and 85.

All plant lists include information regarding specific characteristics that are important to that plant function. These characteristics include fragrance, color, shape, height, spread, soil compaction sensitivity, and seasonal qualities.

The **Soil Compaction Sensitivity** rating system was developed by Gary L. Hightshoe (1988). It is used in the *Climbing & Swinging* (p. 30) and *Shade Quality* (p. 53) plant lists. The term is not precisely defined by Hightshoe, but is used as a general measure of the ability of a particular species to withstand the effects of urban soil compaction. The degree of sensitivity is primarily a function of root structure. Species with shallow, lateral roots are the most sensitive, those with deep lateral roots are more resistant, and those with taproots are most resistant. Sensitivity is also affected by the condition of the soil.

Poisonous plants are discussed in detail in Chapter Three. In addition, plants that appear in the plant lists which have toxic properties are identified with the following abbreviations in the plant lists:

HT = highly toxic   MT = moderately toxic   ST = slightly toxic

These classifications of toxicity are discussed in Chapter Three, as are factors you should keep in mind when deciding when and where you might consider including a plant with known toxic properties in a children's play area. Remember, simply because a plant is "poisonous" does not mean you should necessarily exclude it from consideration.

Seasons are identified in the plant lists using the following abbreviations:

Su = Summer   Sp = Spring   F = Fall   W = Winter

Other abbreviations are footnoted in the tables where they appear.

Sensory Variety

Have you ever stroked a velvety Lamb's Ear? Sniffed a spicy Pink? Heard the clatter of Golden-rain tree pods in the wind?

Children delight in environments that offer a variety of sounds, textures, and smells. Herbs can spellbind children with a wide range of sensations. In particular, many herbs and plants that bear fruits and nuts can stimulate children's taste buds when harvested (see pp. 37-39).

Plants can be selected to provide sensory variety throughout the play environment, or they can be planted together to create a "sensory garden" where children are invited to explore the different smells, tastes, and textures of nature.

Fragrance

Common Name	Botanical Name	Zone	Fragrant Part	Fragrance	Fragrant Season
Ground Covers					
Geranium, Bigroot	*Geranium macrorrhizum*	4 - 8	leaf	geranium	Sp - F
Wintergreen	*Gaultheria procumbens*	3 - 8	crushed leaf	wintergreen	warm weather
Woodruff, Sweet	*Galium odoratum*	5 - 8	crushed leaf, stem	new-mown hay	late Sp - F
Perennials					
Allium					
Giant	*Allium giganteum*	6 - 10	cut/bruised leaf	onion	Sp - F
Ornamental	*Allium spp.*	4 - 10 [1]	cut/bruised leaf	onion	Sp - F
Balm, Bee	*Monarda didyma*	4 - 8	crushed leaf	mint/basil	Sp - F
Chamomile	*Chamaemelum nobile*	3 - 9	leaf	chamomile	Su - F
Daylily	*Hemerocallis spp.*	3 - 9 [1]	flower	varies [1]	early Su - frost [1]
Lily, Fragrant plantain	*Hosta plantaginea*	3 - 9	flower	honey	late Su
Pink, Cottage	*Dianthus plumarius*	4 - 8	flower	spicy	Sp - Su
Snowflake, Spring	*Leucojum vernum*	4 - 8	flower	sweet	early Sp
Thyme, Lemon	*Thymus* x *citriodorus*	5 - 9	leaf, flower	lemon	Sp - F
Shrubs and Trees					
Bayberry	*Myrica pensylvanica*	4 - 9	bruised leaf	spicy	all year
Butterfly bush	*Buddleia davidii*	5 - 9	flower	sweet	July - frost
Cedar, Eastern Red	*Juniperus virginiana*	3 - 9	bark, leaf	cedar	all year
Chaste tree	*Vitex agnus-castus*	6 - 7	flower	sweet	June - July
Cotton, Lavender	*Santolina chamaecyparissus*	6 - 9	bruised leaf	sage	Su
Fern, Sweet	*Comptonia peregrina*	2 - 5	leaf, stem	sweet	all year
Fothergilla					
Dwarf	*Fothergilla gardenii*	6 - 9	flower	honey	April - May
Large	*Fothergilla major*	5 - 9	flower	honey	April - May
Fringe tree	*Chionanthus virginicus*	3 - 9	flower (male)	sweet	May - June

1. *Depends on species or cultivar.*

Fragrance *continued*

Common Name	Botanical Name	Zone	Fragrant Part	Fragrance	Fragrant Season
Shrubs and Trees (contd.)					
Germander, Chamaedrys	*Teucrium chamaedrys*	4 - 9	bruised leaf	pungent	all year
Hawthorn, Yeddo	*Raphiolepis umbellata*	8 - 10	flower	sweet	April
Hazel, Chinese Witch	*Hamamelis mollis*	5 - 9	flower	sweet	Feb - Mar
Jasmine, Poet's	*Jasminum officinale*	7 - 10	dried seed head, flower	jasmine	June - Oct
Juniper					
Hetz Blue	*Juniperus chinensis 'Hetzii'*	4 - 9	leaf	cedar	all year
Pfitzer	*Juniperus chinensis 'Pfitzerana'*	4 - 9	leaf	cedar	all year
Sargent	*Juniperus chinensis var. sargentii*	5 - 9	leaf	cedar	all year
Lavender, English	*Lavandula angustifolia*	5 - 9	flower, leaf	lavender	June - Aug
Magnolia					
Southern	*Magnolia grandiflora*	7 - 9	flower	sweet	May - June
Star	*Magnolia stellata*	5 - 9	flower	sweet	April
Sweet bay	*Magnolia virginiana*	6 - 9	flower	lemon	May - Sept
Myrtle, Wax	*Myrica cerifera*	6 - 9	bruised leaf	spicy	all year
Olive, Russian	*Elaeagnus angustifolia*	2 - 9	silvery flower	gardenia-like	May
Pine (native)					
Eastern White	*Pinus strobus*	4 - 9	needle	pine	all year
Red	*Pinus resinosa*	3 - 6	needle	pine	all year
Pine (non-native)					
Austrian	*Pinus nigra*	5 - 8	needle	pine	all year
Mountain	*Pinus mugo*	3 - 7	needle	pine	all year
Scotch	*Pinus sylvestris*	3 - 7	needle	pine	all year
Rose					
Memorial	*Rosa wichuriana*	5 - 9	flower	rose	late Su
Rugosa	*Rosa rugosa*	4 - 9	flower	rose	June - frost

Fragrance *continued*

Common Name	Botanical Name	Zone	Fragrant Part	Fragrance	Fragrant Season
Shrubs and Trees (contd.)					
Spicebush	*Lindera benzoin*	4 - 9	flower, crushed leaf and stem	spicy	Sp - F
Summer-sweet	*Clethra floridus*	3 - 9	flower	spicy sweet, attracts bees	July - Aug (4-6 wks)
Sweet shrub, Common	*Calycanthus foetidus*	5 - 9	flower, leaf	strawberry	July
Viburnum					
Judd	*Viburnum* x *juddii*	5 - 9	flower	sweet	April - May
Korean spice	*Viburnum carlesii*	6 - 9	flower	sweet	April - May
Wintersweet, Fragrant	*Chimonanthus praecox*	6 - 9	flower	sweet	Dec - Feb
Vines					
Honeysuckle					
Common	*Lonicera periclymenum*	5 - 9	flower	sweet	Su - frost
Etruscan	*Lonicera etrusca 'Superba'*	7 - 9	flower	sweet	Su
Gold Flame	*Lonicera* x *heckrottii*	4 - 9	flower	sweet	late Sp - F
Privet	*Lonicera pileata*	7 - 9	flower	sweet	Sp
Sweet	*Lonicera caprifolium*	6 - 9	flower	sweet	late Sp - Su
Winter	*Lonicera fragrantissima*	5 - 9	flower	sweet	Jan - Mar
Jasmine					
Confederate	*Trachelospermum jasminoides*	8 - 9	flower	sweet	May - June
Yellow Star	*Trachelospermum asiaticum*	7 - 8	flower	sweet	May - June

Note: See also the selection of herbs on pp. 38-39.

Texture

Common Name	Botanical Name	Zone	Part	Texture	Effective Season
Arborvitae, Oriental	*Thuja orientalis*	6 - 9	leaf	reptilian	all year
Cypress, Leyland	x *Cupressocyparis leylandii*	6 - 9	leaf	reptilian	all year
Grass, Fountain	*Pennisetum setaceum*	8 - 10	plume	soft	mid to late Su
Kiwi Fruit	*Actinidia chinensis*	7 - 9	fruit	like stiff suede	Su - F
Lamb's Ears	*Stachys byzantina*	4 - 9	leaf	velvety	Sp - F
Smoke tree, American	*Cotinus obovatus*	3 - 8	flower	feathery	Su
Stonecrop	*Sedum spp.*	4 - 10 [1]	dried seed capsule	woody	persists thru W
Willow, Goat	*Salix caprea*	5 - 8	catkin	like stiff suede	Mar - early Apr

1. *Depends on species or cultivar.*

Wind Effects

Common Name	Botanical Name	Zone	Effective Part	Effect	Effective Season
Birch					
River	*Betula nigra*	4 - 9	leaves	wispy	Sp - F
Sweet	*Betula lenta*	4 - 9	leaves	white underside	Sp - F
Cypress, Common Bald	*Taxodium distichum*	5 - 10	leaves	wispy	Sp - F
Golden-rain tree	*Koelreuteria paniculata*	5 - 9	dried fruit cases leaves	rustling light, airy	persists thru W Sp - F
Grass, Fountain	*Pennisetum setaceum*	8 - 10	leaves plumes	majestic feathery	all year late Su to W
Locust, Thornless Honey	*Gleditsia triacanthos* var. *inermis*	5 - 9	leaves	light, airy	Sp - Su
Maple					
Japanese	*Acer palmatum*	5 - 8	samaras	red, twirling	Sept - Oct
Red	*Acer rubrum*	3 - 9	leaves, samaras	white underside	Sp - F
Money plant	*Lunaria annua*	4 - 9	dried seed cases	papery	Su - W
Variegated	*Lunaria annua* 'Variegata'	4 - 9	dried seed cases	papery	Su - W
Myrtle, Crape	*Lagerstroemia indica*	7 - 10	dried fruit capsule	rustling	persists thru W
Olive, Russian	*Elaeagnus angustifolia*	2 - 9	leaves	silvery underside	Sp - Su
Redwood, Dawn	*Metasequoia glyptostroboides*	4 - 8	leaves	wispy	Sp - F
Viburnum, Double-file	*Viburnum plicatum tomentosum*	5 - 8	leaves	white underside	Sp - F

Play Value

Trees are natural climbing structures. Children of all ages, and even some adults, enjoy the challenge and excitement of climbing among the branches of large trees. However, trees intended for climbing and swinging must be properly located and managed (see note below).

Trees and shrubs also make magnificent hiding places, especially when deliberately chosen and placed for this purpose. Such plantings support chase and hide-and-go-seek games that children love to play. To establish hiding areas, use woody plants that have sparse branches close to the ground and cover a large area. A massing of Viburnums, for instance, creates many spots for hiding.

Probably the most valuable aspect of plants in play areas is the wide variety of play props that naturally drop or can be harvested without harm to the plant. Cones, seeds, pods, leaves, and flowers provide hours of creative recreation when mixed with children's imaginations. Play with plant parts is substantially reinforced if surfaces such as rocks, logs, ledges, and tables are provided above the ground surface.

A Word of Caution

When children climb trees, there is the possibility that they will fall out of them. In today's litigious society, that means possible legal action against the tree's owner. But since children always climb trees, it is perhaps wiser to include climbing trees in the relatively controlled conditions of playgrounds than to have children seek this excitement elsewhere. The listing of suggested species here is not intended to con-done or disapprove of tree climbing. This issue must be resolved local-ly. Designers must check local bylaws regarding trees in public areas and design for safety. Trees with low, horizontal branches should be selected to help climbers feel sky-high with minimal risk, and shock-absorbing surfacing should be installed beneath any tree intended for climbing.

Plants for Play

Climbing and Swinging

Common Name	Botanical Name	Zone	Shape	SCS[1]	Height	Spread
Beech, American	*Fagus grandifolia*	3 - 9	oval	S	50' to 70'	< height
Elm, Chinese	*Ulmus parvifolia*	4 - 9	oval to round	I	40' to 50'	70'
Hackberry, Common	*Celtis occidentalis*	2 - 9	round	I	40' to 60'	40' to 60'
Maple						
Red	*Acer rubrum*	3 - 9	oval to round	R	40' to 60'	3/4 ht.
Sugar	*Acer saccharum*	3 - 8	oval to round	S	60' to 75'	2/3 ht.
Oak						
Sawtooth	*Quercus acutissima*	5 - 9	oval to round	I	35' to 45'	35' to 45'
White	*Quercus alba*	5 - 9	round	S	50' to 80'	50' to 80'
Willow	*Quercus phellos*	5 - 9	oval	R	40' to 60'	30' to 40'
Pagoda tree, Japanese	*Sophora japonica*	5 - 9	spreading	I	50' to 75'	50' to 75'
Pine						
Aleppo	*Pinus halepensis*	9 - 10	conical	R	15' to 40'	10' to 25'
Japanese Black	*Pinus thunbergii*	5 - 8	irregular	R	up to 40'	variable
Italian Stone	*Pinus pinea*	9 - 10	round	R	up to 30'	up to 30'
Pistache, Chinese	*Pistacia chinensis*	6 - 8	oval to round	I	30' to 35'	25' to 35'
Sycamore, Eastern	*Platanus occidentalis*	4 - 9	round	R	75' to 100'	75' to100'
Yellowwood	*Cladrastis lutea*	3 - 8	round	S	30' to 50'	40' to 55'
Zelkova, Japanese	*Zelkova serrata*	5 - 8	vase	R	up to 100'	50' to 80'

1. *Soil Compaction Sensitivity: S = Sensitive; I = Intermediate; R = Resistant*
   See page 21 for description of Soil Compaction Sensitivity rating system.

Hiding Places

Common Name	Botanical Name	Zone	Height	Spread
Bamboo [1]				
Blue Clump	*Semiarundinaria spp.*	7 - 10 [2]	10' to 20' [2]	15' to 30' [2]
Golden-groove	*Phyllostachys aureosulcata*	6 - 10	20' to 25'	spreading
Hedge	*Bambusa glaucescens*	8 - 10	10' to 12'	4' to 6'
Beautyberry, Japanese	*Callicarpa japonica*	5 - 8	4' to 6'	4' to 6'
Birch, Cutleaf European White	*Betula pendula 'Gracilis'*	2 - 6	10' to 15'	10' to 15'
Bottlebrush, Weeping	*Callistemon viminalis 'Red Cascade'*	8 - 10	10' to 25'	10' to 15'
Cranberry bush, European	*Viburnum opulus*	3 - 8	8' to 12'	10' to 15'
Fringe tree	*Chionanthus virginicus*	3 - 9	12' to 20'	12' to 20'
Grass				
Giant Feather	*Stipa gigantea*	7 - 9	up to 8'	tufts
Prairie Cord	*Spartina pectinata*	5 - 9	4' to 6'	spreading
Ravenna	*Erianthus ravennae*	6 - 9	9' to 12'	clump-forming
Silver	*Miscanthus spp.*	4 - 10 [2]	3' to 12' [2]	clump-forming
Switch	*Panicum virgatum*	5 - 9	3' to 6'	spreading
Magnolia, Southern	*Magnolia grandiflora*	7 - 9	60' to 80'	30' to 50'
Maples				
Amur	*Acer ginnala*	6 - 8	15' to 18'	15' to 18'
Hedge	*Acer campestre*	5 - 8	25' to 35'	25' to 35'
Japanese	*Acer palmatum*	5 - 8	15' to 25'	15' to 25'

1. The **Sunset Western Garden Book** *provides an excellent listing of bamboo species on pp. 237-39 of the 1988 edition.*
2. *Depends on species or cultivar.*

Hiding Places *continued*

Common Name	Botanical Name	Zone	Height	Spread
Photinia				
Fraser	*Photinia x fraseri*	8 - 10	6' to 10'	10' to 15'
Japanese	*Photinia glabra*	8 - 10	10' to 12'	15' to 20'
Pittosporum				
Japanese	*Pittosporum tobira*	8 - 10	10' to 15'	spreading
Victorian Box	*Pittosporum undulatum*	9 - 10	15' to 40'	spreading
Smoke tree, American	*Cotinus obovatus*	3 - 8	20' to 30'	10' to 20'
Viburnum				
Black Haw	*Viburnum prunifolium*	3 - 9	12' to 15'	8' to 12'
Double-file	*Viburnum plicatum tomentosum*	5 - 8	8' to 10'	9' to 12'
Willow, Weeping	*Salix babylonica*	6 - 9	30' to 40'	30' to 40'

Play Props

Common Name	Botanical Name	Zone	Play Prop	Height	Spread
Coniferous Trees					
Arborvitae			*cones*		
Giant	*Thuja plicata*	6 - 8	.5" long	50' to 70'	15' to 25'
Oriental	*Thuja orientalis*	6 - 9	.8" long	18' to 25'	10' to 12'
Cypress, Common Bald	*Taxodium distichum*	5 - 10	1" wide	50' to 70'	20' to 30'
Fir			*cones*		
Balsam	*Abies balsamea*	2 - 5	2" to 4" long	45' to 75'	20' to 25'
Fraser	*Abies fraseri*	4 - 7	2.5" long x 2" wide	30' to 40'	20' to 25'
Veitch	*Abies veitchii*	3 - 6	2" long x 1.2" wide	50' to 75'	25' to 35'
Hemlock			*cones*		
Canada	*Tsuga canadensis*	3 - 7	.5" long x 1" wide	40' to 70'	25' to 35'
Carolina	*Tsuga caroliniana*	4 - 7	1.5" long x 1" wide	45' to 60'	20' to 25'
Pine (native)			*cones/needles*		
Eastern White	*Pinus strobus*	4 - 9	6" to 8" long	50' to 80'	20' to 40'
Red	*Pinus resinosa*	3 - 6	2" x 2"	50' to 80'	variable
Pine (non-native)			*cones/needles*		
Austrian	*Pinus nigra*	5 - 8	2" long x 1" wide	50' to 60'	20' to 40'
Mountain	*Pinus mugo*	3 - 7	1.2" long x 1.6" wide	15' to 20'	25' to 30'
Scotch	*Pinus sylvestris*	3 - 7	3" long	30' to 60'	30' to 40'
Spruce			*cones*		
Black	*Picea mariana*	2 - 7	1.5" long	30' to 40'	narrow
Narrow Oriental	*Picea orientalis*	4 - 7	4" long x 1" wide	50' to 60'	up to 15'
White	*Picea glauca*	2 - 6	2.5" long x .75" wide	40' to 60'	10' to 20'

Play Props *continued*

Common Name	Botanical Name	Zone	Play Prop	Height	Spread
Non-Coniferous Trees					
Hazel					
Common Witch	*Hamamelis virginiana*	3 - 8	woody capsule	20' to 30'	20' to 35'
Vernal Witch	*Hamamelis vernalis*	5 - 9	woody capsule	6' to 10'	6' to 10'+
Magnolia					
Saucer	*Magnolia* x *soulangiana*	5 - 9	follicle, flower	20' to 30'	variable
Southern	*Magnolia grandiflora*	7 - 9	leaf, follicle	60' to 80'	30' to 50'
Star	*Magnolia stellata*	5 - 8	flower, follicle	15' to 20'	10' to 15'
Sweet bay	*Magnolia virginiana*	6 - 9	follicle, seed follicle	10' to 30'	10' to 20'
Maple			*paired samaras*		
Amur	*Acer ginnala*	6 - 8	red to brown; 1" long	15' to 18'	15' to 18'
Hedge	*Acer campestre*	5 - 8	1" long	25' to 35'	25' to 35'
Japanese	*Acer palmatum*	5 - 8	red, arched	15' to 25'	15' to 25'
Nikko	*Acer maximowiczianum*	5 - 7	hairy, arched	20' to 30'	20' to 30'
Oak					
Red	*Quercus rubra*	4 - 8	paired, capped nut	60' to 75'	40' to 80'
Water	*Quercus nigra*	7 - 9	capped acorn	50' to 80'	40' to 50'
White	*Quercus alba*	5 - 9	capped nut	<100'	50' to 80'
Willow	*Quercus phellos*	5 - 9	capped nut	40' to 60'	30' to 40'
Pecan	*Carya illinoinensis*	5 - 9	husked edible nut	70' to 100'	40' to 75'
Redbud, Eastern	*Cercis canadensis*	5 - 9	3" pod	20' to 30'	25' to 35'
Silverbell, Carolina	*Halesia carolina*	4 - 8	bell-shaped flower	30' to 40'	20' to 35'
Smoke tree, American	*Cotinus obovatus*	3 - 8	feathery flower	20' to 30'	10' to 20'
Sycamore, Eastern	*Platanus occidentalis*	4 - 9	soft, woody ball	75' to 100'	> height

Play Props *continued*

Common Name	Botanical Name	Zone	Loose Parts	Height	Spread
Perennials					
Lamb's Ears	*Stachys byzantina*	4 - 9	leaf	6" to 12"	24"
Money plant	*Lunaria annua*	4 - 9	seed case	30"	12"
Variegated	*Lunaria annua 'Variegata'*	4 - 9	seed case	30"	12"
Stonecrop	*Sedum spp.*	4 - 10 [1]	dried corymb	2" to 18" [1]	8" to 24" [1]
Shrubs and Grasses					
Bamboo, Heavenly	*Nandina domestica*	7 - 10	red berry	6' to 8'	< height
Bayberry	*Myrica pensylvanica*	4 - 9	waxy, grayish-white berry	9'	5' to 12'
Beautyberry, Purple	*Callicarpa dichotoma*	5 - 8	lilac berry	4' to 6'	4' to 6'
Cranberry bush, European	*Viburnum opulus*	3 - 8	bright red berry	8' to 12'	10' to 15'
Fetterbush	*Pieris floribunda*	5 - 8	flower, capsule	9' to 12'	6' to 8'
Grass					
Feather Reed	*Calamagrostis acutiflora 'Stricta'*	5 - 9	leaf, plume	4'	3'
Fountain	*Pennisetum setaceum*	8 - 10	leaf plume	2' leaves 3' to 4' stems	3'
Reed	*Calamagrostis arundinaceae*	6 - 9	leaf, plume	3'	5'
Myrtle, Wax	*Myrica cerifera*	6 - 9	waxy, grayish-white berry	10' to 15'	10' to 15'

1. *Depends on species or cultivar.*

Play Props *continued*

Common Name	Botanical Name	Zone	Play Prop	Height	Spread
Shrubs and Grasses (contd.)					
Rose-of-Sharon	*Hibiscus syriacus*	5 - 8	flower, capsule	8′ to 12′	6′ to 10′
Skimmia, Japanese	*Skimmia japonica*	7 - 8	red female berry	3′ to 4′	3′ to 4′
Sumac, Fragrant	*Rhus aromatica*	3 - 9	male catkin, red female berry	2′ to 6′	6′ to 10′
Viburnum			*berries*		
Arrowwood	*Viburnum dentatum*	2 - 8	blue berry	6′ to 8′	6′ to 15′
Black Haw	*Viburnum prunifolium*	3 - 9	pink changing to blue	12′ to 15′	8′ to 12′
Double-file	*Viburnum plicatum tomentosum*	5 - 8	red changing to black	8′ to 10′	9′ to 12′
Nannyberry	*Viburnum lentago*	3 - 8	bluish-black	15′ to 18′	6′ to 10
Willow					
Goat	*Salix caprea*	5 - 8	1" long, pinkish-gray catkin	15′ to 25′	12′ to 15′
Pussy	*Salix discolor*	3 - 9	1-1/2" long silver-gray catkin	up to 25'	10' to 15'
Vines					
Akebia, Five-leaf	*Akebia quinata*	4 - 9	pod	20' to 40'	6' to 10'

Nature's Bounty

Plants provide shade, attract birds, and produce beautiful flowers and fragrances. They are even more cherished when they bear fruits, nuts, or seeds to eat. Children love gathering these items.

Herbs and plants that bear fruits, nuts, and seeds can provide valuable educational opportunities in school yards and other programmed environments. They can be used to teach children which plants are edible and which plants are harmful. Of course, plants should be carefully selected and located to avoid putting harmful substances within children's reach. Refer to Chapter Three, *Poisonous Plants and Pesticides*, for more information on this subject. Also, be sure to select insect-resistant varieties so that your pickings will be naturally bigger and better.

Fruits, Herbs & Nuts

Common Name	Botanical Name	Zone	Height	Spread / Form
Fruits				
Blueberry				
Highbush	*Vaccinium corymbosum*	4 - 8	6' to 12'	8' to 12'
Lowbush	*Vaccinium angustifolium*	3 - 7	6" to 2'	8' to 12'
Cherry, Pin	*Prunus pensylvanica*	3 - 8	20' to 35'	20' to 35'
Chokecherry, Common	*Prunus virginiana*	3 - 8	35' to 50'	20' to 35'
Cranberry, American	*Vaccinium macrocarpon*	2 - 6	2' to 6'	indefinite
Currant, Buffalo	*Ribes odoratum*	3 - 8	6' to 8'	6' to 8'
Elderberry, American	*Sambucus canadensis*	3 - 9	6' to 12'	6' to 12'
Kiwi Fruit	*Actinidia chinensis*	7 - 9	vine	indefinite
Mulberry, Red	*Morus rubra*	5 - 9	35' to 50'	35' to 50'
Persimmon, Common	*Diospyros virginiana*	5 - 9	50' to 75'	35' to 50'
Plum, American	*Prunus americana*	3 - 9	20' to 35'	20' to 35'
Pomegranate	*Punica granatum*	7 - 10	12' to 20'	12' to 20'+
Herbs				
Balm, Lemmon	*Melissa officinalis*	4 - 8	up to 2'	spreading
Chamomile	*Chamaemelum nobile*	3 - 9	up to 1'	spreading
Chive	*Allium schoenoprasum*	3 - 10	10" to 18"	clump
Lavender, English	*Lavandula angustifolia*	5 - 9	1' to 3'	clump

Note: It is best to pick herbs in the morning before the sun releases their oils.

Fruits, Herbs & Nuts *continued*

Common Name	Botanical Name	Zone	Height	Spread / Form
Herbs (contd.)				
Geranium	*Pelargonium spp.*	9 - 10	3" to 3'	indefinite
Mint, Pineapple	*Mentha suaveolens 'Variegata'*	5 - 9	18"	spreading
Nasturtium				
Canary Creeper	*Tropaeolum peregrinum*	9 - 10	up to 6"	climber
Garden	*Tropaeolum majus*	5 - 10	up to 2'	spreading
Wreath	*Tropaeolum polyphyllum*	7 - 9	up to 18"	spreading
Oregano	*Origanum vulgare*	5 - 10	18" to 24"	spreading
Peppermint	*Mentha x piperita*	2 - 9	12" to 24"	spreading
Rosemary	*Rosmarinus officinalis*	8 - 10	4' to 6'	4' to 6'
Sage	*Salvia officinalis*	4 - 9	2' to 3'	clump
Spearmint	*Mentha spicata*	2 - 9	1' to 2'	spreading
Thyme				
Common	*Thymus vulgaris*	5 - 9	6" to 12"	6" to 9"
Lemon	*Thymus x citriodorus*	5 - 9	4" to 10"	spreading
Nuts				
Chestnut, Chinese	*Castenea mollissima*	5 - 7	40' to 60'	40' to 60'
Filbert, European	*Corylus avellana*	5 - 10	10' to 15'	10' to 15'
Hazelnut, Western	*Corylus californica*	8 - 10	5' to 12'	5' to 12'
Pecan	*Carya illinoinensis*	5 - 9	70' to 100'	40' to 75'

Seasonal Interest

Autumn's colors are amazing to young children and provide visual testimony to the changing seasons. Winter then presents its own quiet ensemble: cheerful winter berries, exfoliating barks, exquisite patterns of bare branches dusted by newly fallen snow, and handsome evergreens in plush contrast to the starkness of the surrounding landscape. The first few blooms of Spring inspire excitement and promise warmer days ahead.

Fall Color

Common Name	Botanical Name	Zone	Leaf Color
Ash, White	*Fraxinus americana*	4 - 9	yellow
Bamboo, Heavenly	*Nandina domestica*	7 - 10	reddish (persists)
Birch, Sweet	*Betula lenta*	4 - 9	yellow
Dogwood			
Chinese	*Cornus kousa*	5 - 8	red-purple, scarlet
Flowering	*Cornus florida*	5 - 9	red, red-purple
Fothergilla			
Dwarf	*Fothergilla gardenii*	6 - 9	yellow, orange, scarlet
Large	*Fothergilla major*	5 - 9	yellow, orange, scarlet
Gum, American Sweet	*Liquidambar styraciflua*	6 - 9	orange, red, purple
Locust, Thornless Honey	*Gleditsia triacanthos* var. *inermis*	5 - 9	yellow
Maidenhair tree	*Ginkgo biloba*	5 - 9	bright yellow
Maple			
Amur	*Acer ginnala*	6 - 8	red, yellow (red samara)
Hedge	*Acer campestre*	5 - 8	yellow
Japanese	*Acer palmatum*	5 - 8	yellow, bronze, purple, red
Nikko	*Acer maximowiczianum*	5 - 7	red, yellow, purple
Red	*Acer rubrum*	3 - 9	orange-red (variable)
Sugar	*Acer saccharum*	3 - 8	orange, red, yellow
Oak, Red	*Quercus rubra*	4 - 8	russet, wine red
Silverbell, Carolina	*Halesia carolina*	4 - 8	yellow

Fall Color *continued*

Common Name	Botanical Name	Zone	Leaf Color
Smoke tree, American	*Cotinus obovatus*	3 - 8	yellow, red, orange, red-purple
Sourwood	*Oxydendrum arboreum*	5 - 9	red, purple
Spicebush	*Lindera benzoin*	4 - 9	yellow
Spindle tree, Winged	*Euonymus alatus*	3 - 8	pink-scarlet
Summer-sweet	*Clethra alnifolia*	3 - 9	yellow
Tulip tree, American	*Liriodendron tulipifera*	4 - 9	yellow
Viburnum			
Arrowwood	*Viburnum dentatum*	2 - 8	yellow, red, purple
Black Haw	*Viburnum prunifolium*	3 - 9	red, bronze
Double-file	*Viburnum plicatum tomentosum*	5 - 8	red-purple
Linden	*Viburnum dilatatum*	5 - 9	yellow, orange, red
Wintergreen	*Gaultheria procumbens*	3 - 8	reddish (persists)

Winter Berries & Evergreens

Common Name	Botanical Name	Zone	Fruit Color	Fruit Season	Evergreen [1]
Apple, Crab [HT]	*Malus spp.* [2]	4 - 9 [3]	red or yellow	F into W	
Arborvitae					
Giant	*Thuja plicata*	6 - 8	greenish	F into W	EG
Oriental	*Thuja orientalis*	6 - 9	greenish	F into W	EG
Aucuba, Japanese	*Aucuba japonica*	7 - 10	red	F into W	EG
Bamboo, Heavenly	*Nandina domestica*	7 - 10	red	F - W	EG
Barberry					
Japanese	*Berberis thunbergii*	4 - 9	red	F into W	
Korean	*Berberis koreana*	3 - 8	red	F into W	
Paleleaf	*Berberis candidula*	5 - 9	purplish	Aug - Sept	
Bayberry	*Myrica pensylvanica*	4 - 9	gray, waxy	F into W	EG
Cedar, Eastern Red	*Juniperus virginiana*	3 - 9	bluish gray	F into W	EG
Chokeberry, Red	*Aronia arbutifolia*	5 - 9	red	F into W	
Cotoneaster [MT]	*Cotoneaster 'Autumn Fire'*	5 - 8	bright red, orange	F into W	
Cotton, Lavender	*Santolina chamaecyparissus*	6 - 9			EG
Cranberry bush, European	*Viburnum opulus*	3 - 8	red	Oct - Sp	

1. Evergreen trees and shrubs are identified by the abbreviation "EG."
2. For information on the many species and cultivars available see Hériteau, Brickell, and **Sunset Western Garden Book** (pp. 367-69).
3. Depends on species or cultivar.

Winter Berries & Evergreens *continued*

Common Name	Botanical Name	Zone	Fruit Color	Fruit Season	Evergreen
Cypress, Leyland	x *Cupressocyparis leylandii*	6 - 9			EG
Dogwood					
Chinese	*Cornus kousa*	5 - 8	red	Aug - Oct	
Flowering	*Cornus florida*	5 - 9	glossy red	July - Oct	
Fetterbush	*Pieris floribunda*	5 - 8	pearly buds	W - Sp	EG
Fir					
Balsam	*Abies balsamea*	2 - 5	brown	F - W	
Fraser	*Abies fraseri*	4 - 7	brown	F - W	EG
Veitch	*Abies veitchii*	3 - 6	brown	F - W	EG
White	*Abies concolor*	4 - 7	brown	F - W	EG
Fire thorn, Scarlet [MT]	*Pyracantha coccinea*	7 - 8	red	F - W	
Germander, Chamaedrys	*Teucrium chamaedrys*	4 - 9			EG
Hawthorn, Yeddo	*Raphiolepis umbellata*	8 - 10	bluish-black	F - W	EG
Hemlock					
Canada	*Tsuga canadensis*	3 - 7	brown	F - W	EG
Carolina	*Tsuga caroliniana*	4 - 7	brown	F - W	EG
Juniper					
Hetz Blue	*Juniperus chinensis* 'Hetzii'	4 - 9			EG
Pfitzer	*Juniperus chinensis* 'Pfitzerana'	4 - 9			EG
Sargent	*Juniperus chinensis* var. *sargentii*	5 - 9			EG
Lily-of-the-valley bush	*Pieris japonica*	5 - 8	pearly buds	F - W	EG

Winter Berries & Evergreens *continued*

Common Name	Botanical Name	Zone	Fruit Color	Fruit Season	Evergreen
Lilyturf					
Big Blue	*Liriope muscari*	6 - 10	black	F - W	EG
Creeping	*Liriope spicata*	5 - 10	black	F - W	EG
Magnolia					
Southern	*Magnolia grandiflora*	7 - 9	red	F	EG
Sweet bay	*Magnolia virginiana*	6 - 9	red	F	EG
Myrtle					
Pacific Wax	*Myrica californica*	8 - 11	purple	F - W	EG
Wax	*Myrica cerifera*	6 - 9	gray	F - W	EG
Oak, Chinese Evergreen	*Quercus myrsinifolia*	7 - 9	brown	F - W	EG
Photinia					
Chinese	*Photinia serrulata*	7 - 9			EG
Fraser	*Photinia x fraseri*	8 - 10			EG
Japanese	*Photinia glabra*	8 - 10			EG
Pine (native)					
Eastern White	*Pinus strobus*	4 - 9	brown	F - W	EG
Red	*Pinus resinosa*	3 - 6	brown	F - W	EG
Pine (non-native)					
Austrian	*Pinus nigra*	5 - 8	brown	F - W	EG
Mountain	*Pinus mugo*	3 - 7	brown	F - W	EG
Scotch	*Pinus sylvestris*	3 - 7	brown	F - W	EG

Winter Berries & Evergreens *continued*

Common Name	Botanical Name	Zone	Fruit Color	Fruit Season	Evergreen
Skimmia					
Japanese	*Skimmia japonica*	7 - 8	red	Oct - Sp	EG
Reeves	*Skimmia reevesiana*	7 - 9	crimson	W	EG
Spruce					
Black	*Picea mariana*	2 - 7	brown	F - W	EG
Narrow Oriental	*Picea orientalis*	4 - 7	brown	F - W	EG
White	*Picea glauca*	2 - 6	brown	F - W	EG
Viburnum, Leatherleaf	*Viburnum rhytidophyllum*	5 - 9			EG
Wintercreeper	*Eunonymus fortunei*	4 - 9	orange-red	F	EG
Wintergreen	*Gaultheria procumbens*	3 - 8	scarlet	June - Apr	EG

Winter Tracery & Bark

Common Name	Botanical Name	Zone	Shape	Bark
Ash				
Green	*Fraxinus pennsylvanica*	4 - 9	irregular, spreading	ash-gray, furrowed
White	*Fraxinus americana*	4 - 9	open, round	ash-gray, furrowed
Birch				
Paper (White)	*Betula papyrifera*	2 - 6	oval-round	chalky white, exfoliates
River	*Betula nigra*	4 - 9	rounded crown	cinnamon, exfoliates
Dogwood				
Chinese	*Cornus kousa*	5 - 8	vase	mottled, exfoliates
Flowering	*Cornus florida*	5 - 9	tier effect	gray, rectangular blocks
Fringe tree	*Chionanthus virginicus*	3 - 9	spreading, open	gray, smooth, becoming ridged
Katsura tree	*Cercidiphyllum japonicum*	4 - 8	spreading	brown, shaggy
Locust, Thornless Honey	*Gleditsia triacanthos* var. *inermis*	5 - 9	open, round	gray-brown, scaly
Magnolia, Saucer	*Magnolia* x *soulangiana*	5 - 9	pyramidal, spreading	smooth, gray
Maple				
Amur	*Acer ginnala*	6 - 8	rounded	gray-brown
Japanese	*Acer palmatum*	5 - 8	layered	smooth gray
Nikko	*Acer maximowiczianum*	5 - 7	vase	smooth, gray-brown
Paperbark	*Acer griseum*	6 - 8	oval, rounded	cinnamon, exfoliates
Sugar	*Acer saccharum*	3 - 8	upright, round, dense	gray-brown, variable
Myrtle, Crape	*Lagerstroemia indica*	7 - 10	variable	mottled, exfoliates

Winter Tracery & Bark *continued*

Common Name	Botanical Name	Zone	Shape	Bark
Oak				
Pin	*Quercus palustris*	4 - 8	pyramidal	gray-brown
Red	*Quercus rubra*	4 - 8	round top, symmetrical	gray
White	*Quercus alba*	5 - 9	spreading, round	ashy gray, scaly
Pagoda tree, Japanese	*Sophora japonica*	5 - 9	upright, rounded crown	pale gray-brown
Redbud, Eastern	*Cercis canadensis*	5 - 9	spreading, divided trunk	brownish-black
Redwood, Dawn	*Metasequoia glyptostroboides*	4 - 8	pyramidal	red-brown, exfoliates
Silverbell, Carolina	*Halesia carolina*	4 - 8	broad, round crown	gray-black, furrowed
Sycamore, Eastern	*Platanus occidentalis*	4 - 9	open, massive	mottled, white, brown
Tulip tree, American	*Liriodendron tulipifera*	4 - 9	oval-round	brown, furrowed
Willow, Weeping	*Salix babylonica*	6 - 9	weeping, rounded	ridged, furrowed
Yellowwood	*Cladrastis lutea*	3 - 8	round	beech-like
Zelkova, Japanese	*Zelkova serrata*	5 - 8	vase	youth: cherry-like maturity: exfoliates

Winter Flowers

Common Name	Botanical Name	Zone	Flower Color	Season
Camellia, Common	*Camellia japonica*	7 - 9	white, rose, red, & multi-colored	Nov - Apr
Cherry, Cornelian	*Cornus mas*	5 - 8	yellow	Nov - Apr
Fothergilla, Dwarf	*Fothergilla gardenii*	6 - 9	white	early Sp
Hazel, Vernal Witch	*Hamamellis vernalis*	5 - 9	yellow, red	late Jan - Mar
Jasmine, Winter	*Jasminum nudiflorum*	6 - 10	bud: red flower: yellow	Jan - Mar
Wintersweet, Fragrant	*Chimonanthus praecox*	6 - 9	yellow	Dec - Feb

Spring Harbingers

Common Name	Botanical Name	Zone	Flower Color	Season
Apple, Crab [HT]	*Malus spp.* [1]	4 - 9 [2]	white	early Sp
Azalea [HT]	*Rhododendron spp.*	6 - 9 [3]	varies [3]	Sp [3]
Fetterbush	*Pieris floribunda*	5 - 8	white	Apr - May
Fothergilla, Dwarf	*Fothergilla gardenii*	6 - 9	white	early Sp
Glory-of-the-snow	*Chionodoxa luciliae*	3 - 9	blue with white	early Sp
Golden-bells	*Forsythia* x *intermedia*	5 - 9	yellow	early Sp
Hazel, Chinese Witch	*Hamamelis mollis*	5 - 9	red-brown	Mar - Apr
Hyacinth, Grape	*Muscari armeniacum*	2 - 9	blue	early Sp
Lily-of-the-valley bush	*Pieris japonica*	5 - 8	white	Mar - Apr
Magnolia				
Saucer	*Magnolia* x *soulangiana*	5 - 9	white, pink, purple	by mid-Apr
Star	*Magnolia stellata*	5 - 9	white	Mar - Apr
Mimosa, Golden	*Acacia baileyana*	9 - 10	bright yellow	early Sp
Quince, Japanese	*Chaenomeles japonica*	4 - 9	red, orange-red	early Sp
Redbud				
Eastern	*Cercis canadensis*	5 - 9	magenta, pink	mid Sp
Western	*Cercis occidentalis*	8 - 10	magenta	mid Sp

1. *For information on the many species and cultivars available see Hériteau, Brickell, and* **Sunset Western Garden Book** *(pp. 367-69).*
2. *Depends on species or cultivar.*
3. *Depends on species or cultivar. See also Hériteau (pp. 149-53) for further details on azalea cultivars available.*

Spring Harbingers *continued*

Common Name	Botanical Name	Zone	Flower Color	Season
Rhododendron [HT]	*Rhododendron spp.*	4 - 9 [1]	varies [1]	Sp [1]
Skimmia				
Japanese	*Skimmia japonica*	7 - 8	creamy	Mar - Apr
Reeves	*Skimmia reevesiana*	7 - 9	creamy	Apr
Snowflake, Spring	*Leucojum vernum*	4 - 8	white with green	early Sp
Viburnum, Korean Spice	*Viburnum carlesii*	6 - 9	red buds, pink flowers	Mar - Apr
Willow, Goat	*Salix caprea*	5 - 8	1" male catkins	early Sp

1. *Depends on species or cultivar. See also Hériteau (pp. 153-55) for further details on rhododendron species and cultivars available.*

Shade Quality

Large, deciduous trees provide much-needed escape from summer sun and heat. They also add an overhead dimension of "ceilings" that can help differentiate functional areas within the play space. For example, areas with shade ceilings can be designed for quiet play activities or as places where adults can sit while children play in the sun. Shade is also important for children and adults with particular types of disabilities. The design of the play environment should provide a diversity of shaded, semi-shaded, and non-shaded areas to better meet a wide range of needs.

When fully established, shade trees can often be climbed and can serve as swing supports. Since children will naturally play around trees, some protection for the tree's root system may be needed to ensure its growth and stability. This can be provided by spreading a mulch of large woodchips up to twelve inches thick around the base of the tree. This will also help reduce the potential for injury should a child fall from the tree.

The trees listed in the following table vary in height and spread, as well as in the quality of shade provided. However, the typical overall shapes are vase, oval, or round. All listings are deciduous.

Common Name	Botanical Name	Zone	Shape	Shade Quality	SCS [1]
Birch, Sweet	*Betula lenta*	4 - 9	oval to round	moderate	S
Dogwood					
Chinese	*Cornus kousa*	5 - 8	vase to round	light	S
Flowering	*Cornus florida*	5 - 9	round	dense	S
Elm, Chinese	*Ulmus parvifolia*	4 - 9	oval to round	dense	I
Linden, Small-leaved	*Tilia cordata*	3 - 7	oval to round	dense	S
Locust, Thornless Honey	*Gleditsia triacanthos* var. *inermis*	5 - 9	irregular to round	light	R
Maple					
Red	*Acer rubrum*	3 - 9	oval to round	moderate	R
Sugar	*Acer saccharum*	3 - 8	oval to round	dense	S
Mimosa, Silk tree	*Albezia julibrissin*	7 - 10	round	light	R
Oak					
Sawtooth	*Quercus acutissima*	5 - 9	oval to round	dense	I
White	*Quercus alba*	5 - 9	round	moderate	S
Willow	*Quercus phellos*	5 - 9	oval	dense	R
Olive	*Olea europaea*	9 - 10	round, spreading	moderate	R
Pagoda tree, Japanese	*Sophora japonica*	5 - 9	vase	light	I
Pecan	*Carya illinoinensis*	5 - 9	round	light	S
Pistache, Chinese	*Pistacia chinensis*	6 - 8	oval to round	moderate	I
Silverbell, Carolina	*Halesia carolina*	4 - 8	vase to round	dense	S
Sycamore, Eastern	*Platanus occidentalis*	4 - 9	round	light to moderate	R
Yellowwood	*Cladrastis lutea*	3 - 8	round	moderate	S
Zelkova, Japanese	*Zelkova serrata*	5 - 8	vase	dense	R

1. *Soil Compaction Sensitivity: S = Sensitive; I = Intermediate; R = Resistant*
   See page 21 for description of Soil Compaction Sensitivity rating system.

Screens

Evergreen trees and shrubs can provide excellent visual screens and protection from strong winds. Vine-covered fences and densely branched deciduous plants can also serve these purposes.

To create effective wind screens, use several rows of defense. A first row of smaller shrubs can begin to reduce the wind's velocity, while each successive row of shrubs becomes taller and further softens the wind's effects. A final row of trees can seal your area from wind blasts. The screen's range of effectiveness is roughly equal to two times its height (e.g., a screen that is 10' tall will provide protection for a distance of 20' on the leeward side).

A careful match between your requirements and a plant's natural characteristics (height, spread, density) will result in a relatively low-maintenance screen. The plants listed in the following tables tend to grow quickly, resist mildew, and tolerate wind.

Thorny plants can also be used to create physical barriers that enhance the safety of a play area (without compromising aesthetic quality). For example, a dense row of Barberries can be just as effective as a fence in keeping children from wandering into a hazardous area.

Physical Barriers

Common Name	Botanical Name	Zone	Height	Spread
Aralia, Five-leafed	*Acanthopanax sieboldianus*	4 - 9	8' to 10'	8' to 10'
Barberry				
Japanese	*Berberis thunbergii*	4 - 9	3' to 6'	4' to 7'
Korean	*Berberis koreana*	3 - 8	4' to 6'	< ht.
Mentor	*Berberis x mentorensis*	5 - 9	5'	5' to 7'
Paleleaf	*Berberis candidula*	5 - 9	2' to 4'	5'
Wintergreen	*Berberis julianae*	6 - 9	6' to 8'	6' to 8'
Elaeagnus, Thorny	*Elaeagnus pungens*	6 - 9	10' to 15'	10' to 15'
Fire thorn, Scarlet [MT]	*Pyracantha coccinea*	7 - 8	6' to 18'	6' to 18'
Quince, Flowering	*Chaenomeles speciosa*	4 - 9	6' to 10'	6' to 10'
Rose, Rugosa	*Rosa rugosa*	4 - 9	6' to 8'	6' to 8'

*Note: See **Sunset Western Garden Book**, pp. 103 - 105, for additional selections of physical barrier plants.*

Wind Screens & Visual Buffers

Common Name	Botanical Name	Zone	Height	Spread
Arborvitae				
American	*Thuja occidentalis*	3 - 8	40' to 60'	10' to 15'
'Wareana'	*Thuja occidentalis 'Wareana'*	3 - 8	8'	3' to 5'
Cedar, Eastern Red	*Juniperus virginiana*	3 - 9	40' to 50'	8' to 20'
Cypress, Leyland	x *Cupressocyparis leylandii*	6 - 9	60' to 70'	1/4 ht.
Gum tree	*Eucalyptus spp.*[1]	9 - 10	30' to 300'	20' to 50'
Hemlock				
Canada	*Tsuga canadensis*	3 - 7	40' to 70'	25' to 35'
Carolina	*Tsuga caroliniana*	4 - 7	45' to 60'	20' to 25'
Oak, Laurel	*Quercus imbricaria*	4 - 8	50' to 60'	50' to 60'
Photinia				
Chinese	*Photinia serrulata*	7 - 9	20' to 30'	2/3 ht.
Fraser	*Photinia* x *fraseri*	8 - 10	10' to 15'	1/2 ht.
Japanese	*Photinia glabra*	8 - 10	10' to 12'	8' to 10'
Pine, Eastern White	*Pinus strobus*	4 - 9	50' to 80'	20' to 40'
Spruce				
Norway	*Picea abies*	2 - 7	40' to 60'	25' to 30'
Serbian	*Picea omorika*	4 - 7	50' to 60'	20' to 25'
Viburnum, Leatherleaf	*Viburnum rhytidophyllum*	5 - 9	10' to 15'	10' to 15'

Note: See **Sunset Western Garden Book**, *pp. 108 - 109, for additional selection of screen plants.*

1. *Numerous species are available; Flowering Gum (Eucalyptus ficifolia) and Silver-Dollar Tree (Eucalyptus cinerea) are especially interesting for play areas.*

Wildlife Enhancement

For children to become environmentally aware, they must be able to see how plants feed and shelter animals. Birds flock to berries and seeds, squirrels scurry to acorns, and butterflies flutter to flowers full of nectar. Vegetation provides habitat for a myriad of insects, anthropods, arachnids, and other small organisms that fascinate children.

Perhaps you can dedicate a specific part of your play yard for a caterpillar/butterfly garden; or place a bird sanctuary outside a window where birds can be identified for winter education. These "nature gardens" take a relatively small area, yet produce hours of contentment and education for children as well as adults.

Here is a list of trees and shrubs that will coax animals into your playground.[1]

1. There are a number of excellent references that provide additional information and lists of plants that attract wildlife. They include: Calloway Gardens' **Butterfly Gardening**, Peter Cawdell's **Starting a Butterfly Garden**, Rosalind Creasy's **Earthly Delights** (pp. 89-97), Michael Dirr's **Manual of Woody Landscape Plants** (pp. 59-60), Jacqueline Hériteau's **National Arboretum Book of Outstanding Garden Plants** (pp. 43-46, 135, 180, 227), Nigel Matthews' **Garden for Birds**, and the **Sunset Western Garden Book** (pp. 154-155). All of these sources are listed in the Annotated Bilbliography at the end of this book.

Common Name	Botanical Name	Zone	Wildlife Users
Very High Wildlife Value			
Abelia	*Abelia chinensis*	5 - 9	butterflies
Birch			
Gray	*Betula populifolia*	4 - 7	song & water birds, small mammals, browsers
Paper (White)	*Betula papyrifera*	2 - 6	song & upland groundbirds, small mammals, hoofed browsers
River	*Betula nigra*	4 - 9	songbirds, waterfowl, small mammals, browsers
Sweet	*Betula lenta*	4 - 9	song & upland groundbirds, small mammals, browsers
Blueberry			
Highbush	*Vaccinium corymbosum*	4 - 8	song & upland gamebirds, waterfowl, small mammals, browsers, waterfowl
Lowbush	*Vaccinium angustifolium*	3 - 7	songbirds, waterfowl, upland gamebirds, marshbirds, large & small mammals
Butterfly bush	*Buddleia davidii*	5 - 9	hummingbirds and butterflies
Cedar, Eastern Red	*Juniperus virginiana*	3 - 9	song & upland groundbirds, small mammals, hoofed browsers
Dogwood, Flowering	*Cornus florida*	5 - 9	song & upland groundbirds, small mammals, hoofed browsers, waterbirds, large mammals
Maple			
Red	*Acer rubrum*	4 - 9	song & waterbirds, small mammals, browsers
Sugar	*Acer saccharum*	3 - 8	song & upland groundbirds, small mammals, hoofed browsers
Oak, White	*Quercus alba*	5 - 9	song & upland groundbirds, small mammals, hoofed browsers

Common Name	Botanical Name	Zone	Wildlife Users
Very High Wildlife Value (contd.)			
Pine			
Eastern White	*Pinus strobus*	4 - 9	song & upland groundbirds, small mammals, hoofed browsers
Red	*Pinus resinosa*	3 - 6	song & upland groundbirds, small mammals, hoofed browsers
Spicebush	*Lindera benzoin*	4 - 9	song & upland gamebirds, white-tail deer
Sumac, Fragrant	*Rhus aromatica*	3 - 9	upland gamebirds, large & small mammals, hoofed browsers
High Wildlife Value			
Fir			
Balsam	*Abies balsamea*	2 - 5	songbirds, small mammals, hoofed browsers
White	*Abies concolor*	4 - 7	songbirds, small mammals, hoofed browsers
Spruce			
Black	*Picea mariana*	2 - 7	songbirds, small mammals, hoofed browsers
White	*Picea glauca*	2 - 6	songbirds, small mammals, hoofed browsers
Viburnum, Double-file	*Viburnum plicatum tomentosum*	5 - 8	upland gamebirds, songbirds
Intermediate Wildlife Value			
Fringe tree	*Chionanthus virginicus*	3 - 9	small mammals, songbirds
Hemlock, Canada	*Tsuga canadensis*	3 - 7	small mammals, songbirds
Pecan	*Carya illinoinensis*	5 - 9	songbirds

Note: Wildlife species prefer indigenous plants but will gradually grow accustomed to non-natives.

Erosion Control

    Play areas are often relegated to marginal land with steep slopes or poor drainage. Both weather and children at play can cause significant erosion on these sites.

    Plants can play an important role in reducing erosion in play areas. For example, groundcovers for large and small areas can help reduce erosion caused by water, wind, and the feet of children at play. Likewise, large, broad-leaved deciduous trees can help reduce the impact of heavy rain on ground surfaces, extending the runoff time and promoting percolation of water back into the ground. The roots of such trees also help stabilize soils on hillsides and insulate loose soil from precipitation and wind. Trees and shrubs used as windbreaks can also mitigate the erosive effects of wind (see page 56 for a list of plants that make good wind screens).

Common Name	Botanical Name	Zone	Height	Spread
Akebia, Five-leaf	*Akebia quinata*	4 - 9	20' to 40'	twining climber
Bayberry	*Myrica pensylvanica*	4 - 9	5' to 12'	5' to 12'
Dogwood, Tartarian	*Cornus alba*	2 - 8	8' to 10'	5' to 10'
Fern, Sweet	*Comptonia peregrina*	2 - 5	2' to 4'	4' to 8'
Forsythia				
Border	*Forsythia* x *intermedia*	5 - 9	8' to 10'	10' to 12'
Weeping	*Forsythia suspensa*	6 - 8	8' to 10'	10' to 15'
Jasmine, Winter	*Jasminum nudiflorum*	6 - 10	up to 10'	up to 10'
Juniper, Sargent	*Juniperus chinensis* var. *sargentii*	3 - 9	18" to 2'	7.5' to 9'
Myrtle, Wax	*Myrica cerifera*	6 - 9	10' to 15'	5' to 15'
Periwinkle, Dwarf	*Vinca minor*	4 - 8	3" to 6"	5'
Rose, Memorial	*Rosa wichuriana*	5 - 9	trailing vine	15' to 30'
Spurge, Japanese	*Pachysandra terminalis*	4 - 8	4"	spreading
Sumac, Fragrant	*Rhus aromatica*	3 - 9	2' to 6'	6' to 10'
Summer-sweet	*Clethra alnifolia*	3 - 9	3' to 8'	4' to 6'
Viburnum				
Arrowwood	*Viburnum dentatum*	2 - 8	6' to 8'	6' to 15'
Nannyberry	*Viburnum lentago*	3 - 8	15' to 18'	6' to 10'

Note: Hériteau, p. 113, provides additional listings of ground covers useful for erosion control.

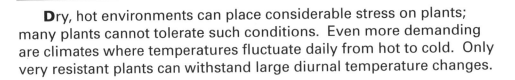
Drought Tolerance

Dry, hot environments can place considerable stress on plants; many plants cannot tolerate such conditions. Even more demanding are climates where temperatures fluctuate daily from hot to cold. Only very resistant plants can withstand large diurnal temperature changes.

Many plant species have characteristics such as deep root systems and fleshy, waxy, or hairy leaves that help them withstand grueling heat, limited water, and sudden drops in temperature. Such plants are valuable resources for play areas in extreme climates. They also offer valuable education opportunities. Native species can be used to teach children about nature's adaptations to local conditions and to introduce concepts such as water conservation.

Locating plants in cooler, moist micro-climates (under shade trees, beside a pond) can bolster stability. Even the hardiest plants will react positively to such protection in harsh climates.

Common Name	Botanical Name	Zone	Tolerances[1]		
			Cold	Heat	Drought
Shrubs					
Bayberry	*Myrica pensylvanica*	4 - 9	R	R	R
Blueberry					
Highbush	*Vaccinium corymbosum*	4 - 8	R	R	R
Lowbush	*Vacinnium angustifolium*	3 - 7	R	R	R
Buffalo berry	*Shepherdia canadensis*	2 - 7	R	R	R
Ceanothus	*Ceanothus spp.* [2]	3 - 9[3]	R	R	R
Cinquefoil, Shrubby	*Potentilla fruticosa*	3 - 8	R	R	R
Fothergilla					
Dwarf	*Fothergilla gardenii*	6 - 9	I	I	I
Large	*Fothergilla major*	5 - 9	I	I	I
Juniper					
Hetz Blue	*Juniperus chinensis 'Hetzii'*	4 - 9	R	R	R
Pfitzer	*Juniperus chinensis 'Pfitzerana'*	4 - 9	R	R	R
Sargent	*Juniperus chinensis* var. *sargentii*	5 - 9	R	R	R
Lilac					
Common	*Syringa vulgaris*	5 - 8	R	R	R
Persian	*Syringa persica*	5 - 9	R	R	R

1. *Tolerances: R = Resistant; I = Intermediate resistance.*
2. *Many Caenothus species and cultivars are available, particularly on the West Coast. The* **Sunset Western Garden Book** *provides a good list on pp. 271-72.*
3. *Depends on species or cultivar.*

Common Name	Botanical Name	Zone	Tolerances [1]		
			Cold	*Heat*	*Drought*
Shrubs (contd.)					
Rose					
Carolina	*Rosa carolina*	4 - 9	I	R+	R+
Rugosa	*Rosa rugosa*	4 - 9	R	R	R
Summer-sweet	*Clethra alnifolia*	3 - 9	R	I	I
Viburnum					
Black Haw	*Viburnum prunifolium*	3 - 9	R	R	R
Nannyberry	*Viburnum lentago*	3 - 8	R	R	R
Wintergreen	*Gaultheria procumbens*	3 - 8	R	I	I
Trees					
Ash					
Green	*Fraxinus pennsylvanica*	4 - 9	R	R	R
White	*Fraxinus americana*	4 - 9	R	I	I
Birch					
Gray	*Betula populifolia*	4 - 7	R	R	R
River	*Betula nigra*	4 - 9	I	R	R
Sweet	*Betula lenta*	4 - 9	R	I	I
Cedar, Eastern Red	*Juniperus virginiana*	3 - 9	R	R	R
Dogwood, Flowering	*Cornus florida*	5 - 9	I	I	I
Elder, Box	*Acer negundo*	3 - 9	R	R	R

1. *Tolerances: R = Resistant; I = Intermediate resistance.*

Trees (contd.)

Common Name	Botanical Name	Zone	Tolerance [1]		
			Cold	*Heat*	*Drought*
Golden-rain tree	*Koelreuteria paniculata*	5 - 9	I	R	R
Hackberry, Common	*Celtis occidentalis*	2 - 9	R	R	R
Hornbeam					
American	*Carpinus caroliniana*	3 - 9	R	R	R
European	*Carpinus betulus*	5 - 9	I	I	R
Locust					
Black *MT*	*Robinia pseudoacacia*	4 - 9	R	R	R
Idaho	*Robinia ambigua 'Idahoensis'*	5 - 9	R	R	R
Thornless Honey	*Gleditsia triacanthos* var. *inermis*	5 - 9	R	R	R
Maidenhair tree	*Ginkgo biloba*	5 - 9	R	R	R
Maple					
Hedge	*Acer campestre*	5 - 8	R	R	R
Norway	*Acer platanoides*	4 - 7	R	R	R
Red	*Acer rubrum*	4 - 9	R	I	I
Trident	*Acer buergerianum*	5 - 9	R	R	R
Mulberry, Paper	*Broussonetia papyrifera*	7 - 9	R	R	R
Olive, Russian	*Elaeagnus angustifolia*	2 - 9	R	R	R
Pagoda tree, Japanese	*Sophora japonica 'Regent'*	5 - 9	R	R	R

1. *Tolerances: R = Resistant; I = Intermediate resistance.*

Common Name	Botanical Name	Zone	Tolerances [1]		
			Cold	*Heat*	*Drought*
Trees (contd.)					
Pecan	*Carya illinoinensis*	5 - 9	I	I	I
Pine, Red	*Pinus resinosa*	3 - 6	R	I	I
Redbud, Eastern	*Cercis canadensis*	5 - 9	I	R	R
Smoke tree, American	*Cotinus obovatus*	3 - 8	I	R	R
Sourwood	*Oxydendrum arboreum*	5 - 9	I	I	I
Spruce					
Black	*Picea mariana*	2 - 7	R	R	R
White	*Picea glauca*	2 - 6	R	R	R
Sycamore, Eastern	*Platanus occidentalis*	4 - 9	I	R	R

1. *Tolerances: R = Resistant; I = Intermediate resistance.*

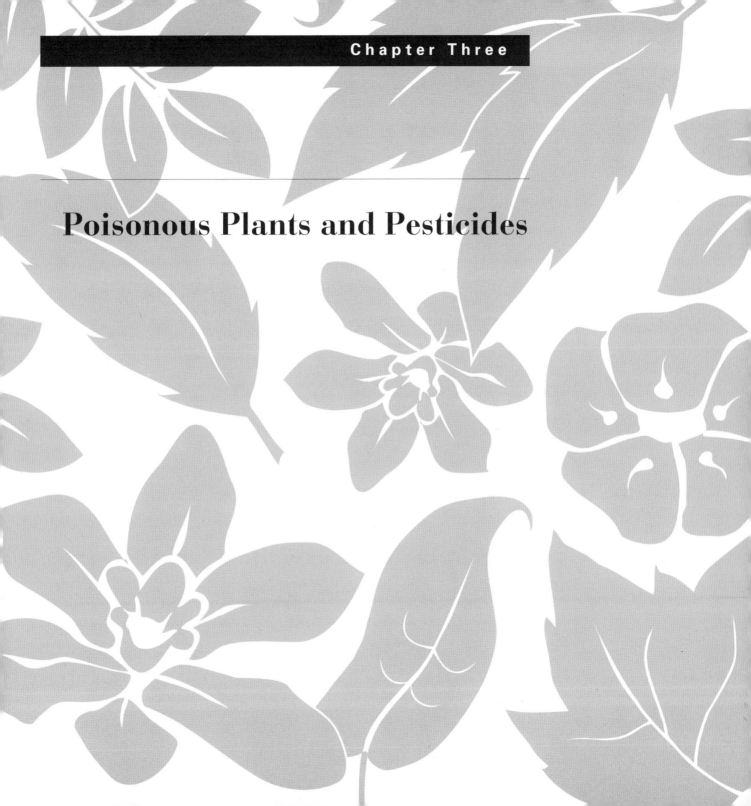

Chapter Three

Poisonous Plants and Pesticides

About Poisonous Plants

The great majority of plants are highly beneficial and perfectly safe for children's play areas. However, there are a number of naturally occurring poisons in the plant world, some of which are highly concentrated in certain plant species. Some of these poisons can be dangerous to humans if ingested while others can cause dermatitis or other allergic reactions. For example, one or two seeds from a castor bean plant (*Ricinus communis*), if chewed and swallowed, could be deadly to a young child.

Nonetheless, children rarely die from plant poisons. In 1989, the latest year for which statistics are available, only one child in the under 5 year old group died from plant poisoning in the United States. No children in the 5 to 14 year old group died.[1] The *American Medical Association Handbook of Poisonous and Injurious Plants* indicates that most cases of plant ingestion are the result of very young children eating parts of *indoor* plants.

Depending on the species, poisons may be found throughout various plant parts or may be concentrated in one part. That is why it is possible to eat the harmless petioles of rhubarb (*Rheum rhabarbarum*) but not the poisonous leaf blades. Likewise, some plant parts that are poisonous when raw or unripe are edible when cooked or ripened. For example, the poison found in the roots of certain kinds of cassava (*Manihot*), a staple food in many parts of the world, is dispelled when cooked.

Because of the complex nature of poisonous plants, it is not necessarily the best policy to ban them altogether from your play area. Most

1. National Safety Council, **Accident Facts** *(Itasca, IL: National Safety Council, 1992), p. 98.*

plant poisons can act only if ingested, and the seriousness of reaction depends on the amount eaten. For example, apple (*Malus*) seeds are poisonous, but a child would have to eat a large number of apple seeds to fall seriously ill. It would be an extreme reaction to keep children away from apples as a means of protecting them from these toxic seeds.

The actual risk of children being harmed by plants outdoors can be minimized if reasonable precautions are taken when selecting plant species and locating them in children's outdoor play environments. The best approach is to familiarize yourself with plants that have poisonous properties and to take preventative measures. The list of plant species on the following pages will help you quickly identify some of the more common plants in which poisons are found. These plants are listed by botanical name to avoid the possibility of confusion with other plant species. Additional information can be found in several of the sources listed in the annotated bibliography at the end of this book. Your local agricultural extension service office or poison control center can also provide useful information.

In addition to increasing your knowledge of poisonous plants, you should consider the following:

Age of Children. The age of the children who will be using your play area should be considered when selecting and locating plants. Greater care must be taken with regard to toxic plants in areas used by infants and toddlers, since these age groups are likely to put plant parts in their mouths if given the opportunity. Avoid placing highly toxic plants, particularly plants with poisonous fruits and plants that can cause dermatitis, within reach of these age groups. Of equal concern are plants with small seeds or berries that very young children could choke on.

Educational Benefits. Children will come across poisonous plants at some point during their childhood. If they are unaware of what those plants look like and the dangers they represent, there is a greater possibility that they may expose themselves to those dangers. School yards and other supervised environments provide opportunities for teaching children about plants that are poisonous. I remember well the lessons I received about "deadly nightshade" (*Solanum nigrum*) when I was growing up in rural England. I can recognize the plant in an instant even today. You may want to purposely include different types of common poisonous plants in your planting design to support such educational opportunities. Depending on the species you choose, you may want to label or group these plants together.

Supervision and Prevention. The best method of prevention is to teach children not to put any plant or plant part into their mouth that they cannot positively identify as good, wholesome food. Selected plantings of edible species (as listed in *Nature's Bounty* on pages 38 and 39) can help children identify plants that are good to eat so that they can avoid all others. In addition, supervisory staff should be aware of which plants in the play area have poisonous properties and should keep younger children away from them. If a poisonous plant is ingested, a physician should be consulted immediately. The phone number of a physician and/or your local or regional Poison Control Center should be kept next to your phone for such emergencies.

About Pesticides

There are many more children that fall ill each year from exposure to pesticides than from ingesting natural plant poisons. Improper pest management and weed control practices can make all of the plants in your play area, including edible species, poisonous.

To the extent possible, you should employ natural methods of pest management and weed control. These can include selection of pest- and disease-resistant plant species and the use of mechanical controls such as a strong jet of water to literally wash pests off, removal of plant debris that attracts pests, or good old-fashioned weeding by hand. Nonchemical pest management alternatives include release or encouragement of beneficial insects and use of botanical insecticides such as natural pyrethrins.

If you have to resort to chemical preparations, do so only with great care. Follow label directions exactly and do not let children use the area until it is absolutely safe. If misused, chemical pesticides can damage your plants and pose an environmental hazard. However, use of such pesticides may be necessary to address large-scale infestations.

For more information on pest management and weed control in your locale, consult a professional at a reputable local nursery, a horticultural consultant, or the agriculture department at a nearby university. There are also several references listed at the end of this book.

About the Lists

The following list is organized in three sections: Highly Toxic Plants, Moderately Toxic Plants, and Slightly Toxic Plants. **Highly Toxic Plants** are those species that are known to cause serious illness or (in extreme cases) death when ingested. **Moderately Toxic Plants** include those species that can cause illness when ingested or serious contact dermatitis. **Slightly Toxic Plants** are species that cause mild illness or contact dermatitis. Remember, however, that the seriousness of reaction depends in large part on the amount of plant material eaten as well as the condition and tolerances of the person affected. Young children are likely to have more pronounced responses to plant toxins than adults simply because they are smaller in size.

The plants listed here are among the more common species of poisonous plants. However, it is not a comprehensive list. There are over 700 plants in North America that are known to be poisonous to humans or animals. The *American Medical Association Handbook of Poisonous and Injurious Plants* by Kenneth Lampe (see Chapter Six, *Annotated Bibliography*) is an excellent reference for a more comprehensive treatment of this subject.

Highly Toxic Plants

Botanical Name	Common Name	Toxic Parts
Abrus precatorius	Rosary pea	seeds
Acokanthera spp. [Carissa spectabilis]	Poison bush, Wintersweet	fruit and plant
Aconitum napellus	Monkshood	all parts
Alocasia macrorrhiza	Taro	all parts
Atropa belladona	Belladonna	all parts
Conium maculatum	Hemlock	all parts
Convallaria majalis	Lily-of-the-valley	all parts
Daphne spp.	Daphne	berries, bark
Datura spp.	Angel's trumpet	nectar, seeds
Delphinium spp.	Larkspur	all parts
Dieffenbachia spp.	Dumb cane	berries
Duranta repens	Golden-dewdrop	berries
Euphorbia pulcherrima	Poinsettia	sap
Euphorbia spp.	Spurges	sap
Gloriosa superba	Glory lily	all parts, esp. root

Highly Toxic Plants *continued*

Botanical Name	Common Name	Toxic Parts
Ilex aquifolium	English holly	fruits and leaves
Ilex opaca	American holly	fruits and leaves
Jatropha spp.	Coral plant, Barbados nut, Physic nut	seeds
Kalmia spp.	Laurels	all parts
Laburnum anagyroides	Golden-chain tree	all parts
Lantana spp.	Lantana	green fruits
Ligustrum spp.	Privet	fruit
Lobelia cardinalis	Cardinal flower	all parts
Malus spp.	Apple	leaves, seeds in large amounts
Melia azedarach	Bead tree, Chinaberry	fruit, leaf, bark and flowers
Nerium oleander	Oleander	all parts
Nicotiana glauca	Tree tabacco	all parts, esp.leaves
Prunus spp.	Apricot, Peach, Bitter almond	kernel, flower, leaf, bark
Rheum rhabarbarum	Rhubarb	leaf blade

Highly Toxic Plants *continued*

Botanical Name	Common Name	Toxic Parts
Rhododendron spp.	Rhododendrons, Azaleas	leaf
Ricinus communis	Castor bean plant	seeds (2 - 8)
Solanum dulcamara	Nightshade	all parts
Solanum nigrum	Nightshade	green fruit
Solanum psedocapsicum	Jerusalem cherry	berries
Solanum sodomeum`	Apple-of-Sodom	fruit
Solanum tuberosum	Potato	green skin
Tabernaemontana divaricata	Crape jasmine	all parts
Taxus spp.	Yews	all parts, esp. seed in pod
Thevetia peruviana	Yellow oleander	all parts, esp. seed in kernel
Wisteria spp.	Wisteria	seeds and pods
Zantedeschia aethiopica	Arum lily, Calla lily	all parts, esp. juice of leaves & stem

Moderately Toxic Plants

Botanical Name	Common Name	Toxic Parts
Aesculus spp.	Buckeye, Horse chestnut	all parts
Aleurites fordii	Tung-oil tree	fruit kernel
Allamanda spp.	Allamanda	fruit
Amaryllis belladonna	Lily, Belladonna	bulb
Anemone spp.	Windflower	all parts
Aquilegia spp.	Columbine	seeds
Arum italicum	Italian arum	sap, esp. berries
Arum maculatum	Lords-and-ladies	sap
Asclepias fruticosa	Swan plant	pods
Caladium spp.	Caladium	all parts
Castanospermum australe	Black bean, Moreton bay chestnut	seeds
Celastrus spp.	Bittersweet	all parts
Cestrum spp.	Day-blooming cestrum, Jessamine	all parts, esp. fruit
Chrysanthemum morifolium	Florist's Chrysanthemum	all parts
Colocasia spp.	Elephant's-ear	root
Colocasia esculenta	Taro root	root

Moderately Toxic Plants *continued*

Botanical Name	Common Name	Toxic Parts
Cotoneaster spp.	Cotoneaster	fruit, flowers
Crataegus spp.	Hawthorn	fruit
Cydonia oblonga	Quince	seeds, fresh leaves
Digitalis purpurea	Foxglove	all parts
Eriobotrya japonica	Loquat	seeds
Euonymus europaea	European spindle tree	all parts, esp. fruit and seeds
Gelsemium sempervirens	Yellow jessamine	all parts
Hedera helix	English ivy	all parts, esp. berries
Hura crepitans	Sandbox tree	all parts
Hyacinthus orientalis	Hyacinth	all parts, exp. bulb
Hydrangea spp.	Hydrangea	flowers
Iris germanica	Flag, Fleur-de-lis	all parts
Lupinus spp.	Lupine	seed pods
Manihot esculenta	Cassava	raw roots
Moraea spp.	Iris, Butterfly	all parts
Narcissus jonquilla	Jonquil	sap and bulb

Moderately Toxic Plants *continued*

Botanical Name	Common Name	Toxic Parts
Narcissus pseudonarcissus	Daffodil	sap and bulb
Nerine spp.	Spider lily	bulb
Ornithogalum arabicum	Star-of-Bethlehem	bulb or flower spike
Ornithogalum thyrsoides	Chincherinchee	bulb or flower spike
Philodendron spp.	Philodendron	all parts
Physalis alkelengi	Ground cherry	unripe fruit
Physalis ixocarpa	Tomatillo, Chinese lantern	unripe fruit
Plumeria spp.	Frangipani	sap
Poinciana gilliesii	Bird-of-paradise plant	unripe seed pod
Prunus cerasus	Pie cherry, Sour cherry	kernels
Prunus laurocerasus	Laurel cherry	bruised leaves
Pyrus communis	Pear	seeds
Rhamnus spp.	Buckthorn, Cascara sagrada	fruit
Robinia pseudoacacia	Black locust	all parts
Solandra spp.	Golden chalice, Gold cup	sap, leaves, flowers
Solanum aviculare	Kangaroo apple	green fruit

Moderately Toxic Plants *continued*

Botanical Name	Common Name	Toxic Parts
Schinus molle	Pepper tree	fruit
Schinus terebinthifolius	Brazilian pepper tree	fruit, large amounts
Hyacinthoides non-scriptus	English bluebell	all parts
Scilla peruviana	Cuban lily, Hyacinth-of-Peru	all parts

Slightly Toxic Plants

Botanical Name	Common Name	Toxic Parts
Achillea millefolium	Milfoil, Common yarrow	all parts
Agapanthus africanus	African blue lily	sap
Artemisia absinthium	Common wormwood	all parts
Chrysanthemum coccineum	Pyrethrum	all parts
Chrysanthemum parthenium	Feverfew	all parts
Clematis spp.	Traveller's joy	all parts
Colchicum autumnale	Autumn crocus	flowers
Cosmos bipinnatus	Cosmos	all parts
Cotinus coggygria	Smoke Tree	sap
Cycas spp.	Zamia palm	seeds, fresh or improperly prepared
Dicentra spectabilis	Bleeding heart	all parts
Echium lycopsis	Paterson's curse	all parts
Helenium autumnale	Sneezeweed	all parts
Helianthus annuus	Sunflower	all parts
Monstera deliciosa	Fruit salad, Swiss cheese plant	ripe fruit
Primula obconica	Primula	all parts

Slightly Toxic Plants *continued*

Botanical Name	Common Name	Toxic Parts
Ranunculus spp.	Buttercups	all parts
Rhus radicans	Poison ivy	all parts
Rhus vernix	Poison sumac	all parts
Rudbeckia hirta	Black-eyed-Susan	all parts
Senecio cineraria	Dusty miller	all parts
Tanacetum vulgare	Common tansy	all parts
Urtica spp.	Stinging nettle	all parts

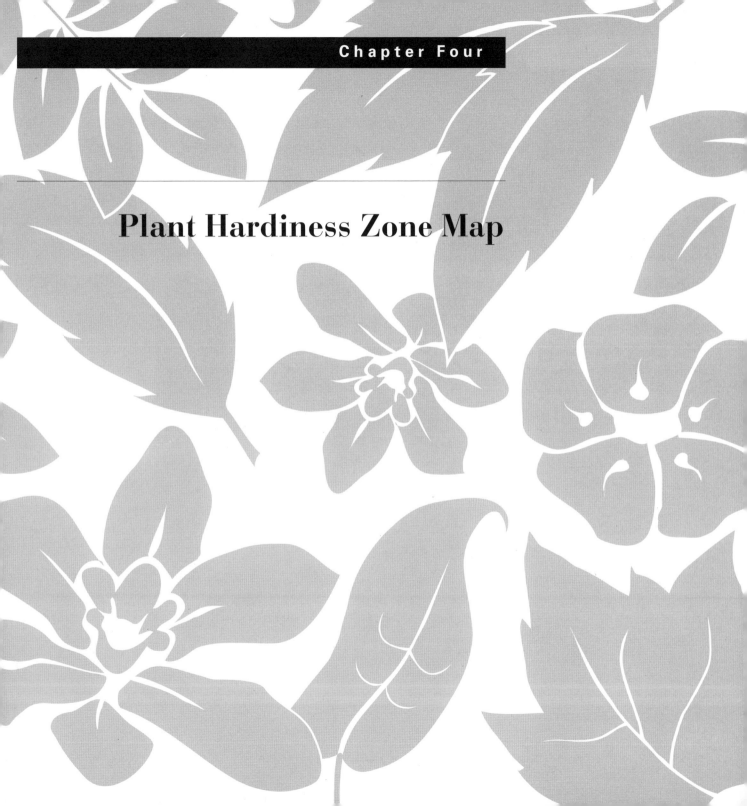

Chapter Four

Plant Hardiness Zone Map

The map below and on the following page identifies the plant hardiness zones of the U.S. All of the plants listed in this book are identified by zone to help you select plants that are appropriate for your area.

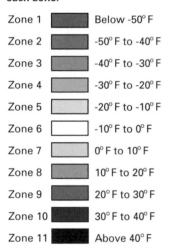

Range of average annual minimum temperatures for each zone.

Zone 1		Below -50° F
Zone 2		-50° F to -40° F
Zone 3		-40° F to -30° F
Zone 4		-30° F to -20° F
Zone 5		-20° F to -10° F
Zone 6		-10° F to 0° F
Zone 7		0° F to 10° F
Zone 8		10° F to 20° F
Zone 9		20° F to 30° F
Zone 10		30° F to 40° F
Zone 11		Above 40° F

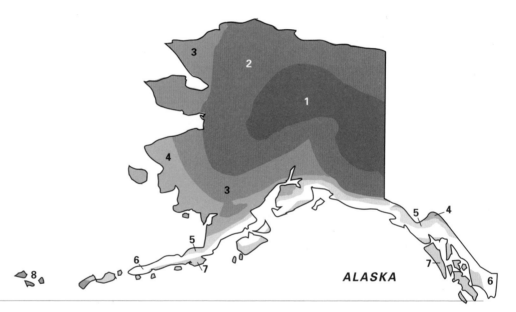

ALASKA

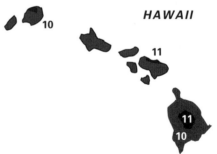

HAWAII

If your location is not shown on the map, use the temperature ranges to determine the appropriate zone designation.

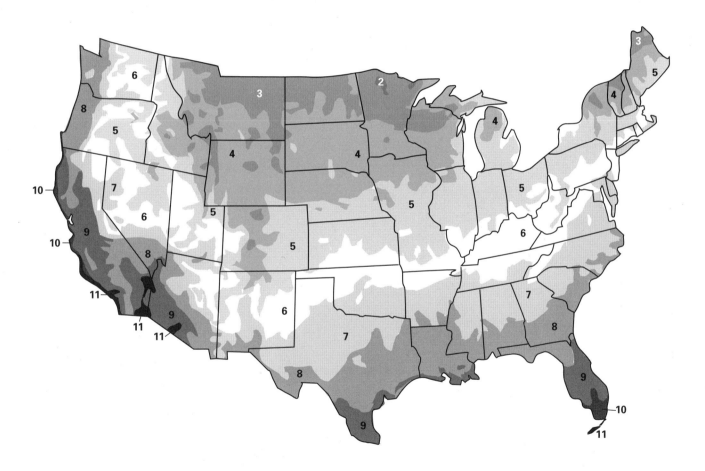

Source: United States Department of Agriculture, 1990

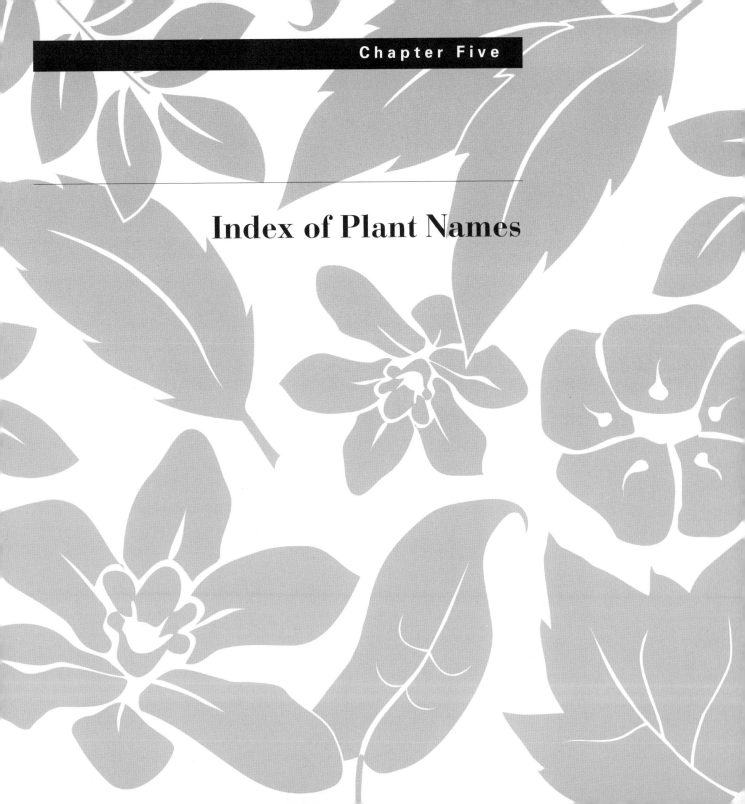

Chapter Five

Index of Plant Names

Plant Functions

Fragrance (p. 24-26)	Texture (p. 27)	Wind Effects (p. 28)	Climbing & Swinging (p. 30)	Hiding Places (p. 31-32)	Play Props (p. 33-36)	Fruits, Herbs & Nuts (p. 38-39)	Fall Color (p. 41-42)	Winter Berries & Evergrns. (p. 43-46)	Winter Tracery & Bark (p. 47-48)	Winter Flowers (p. 49)	Spring Harbingers (p. 50-51)	Shade Quality (p. 53)	Physical Barriers (p. 55)	Wind Screens/Visual Buffers (p. 56)	Wildlife Enhancement (p. 58-59)	Erosion Control (p. 61)	Drought Tolerance (p. 63-66)	
															●			**Abelia** *Abelia chinensis*
					●											●		**Akebia, Five-leaf** *Akebia quinata*
●																		**Allium** — Giant — *Allium giganteum*
●																		Ornamental — *Allium spp.*
								●			●							**Apple, Crab** HT — *Malus spp.*
													●					**Aralia, Five-leafed** *Acanthopanax sieboldianus*
														●				**Arborvitae** — American — *Thuja occidentalis*
					●			●										Giant — *Thuja plicata*
	●				●			●										Oriental — *Thuja orientalis*
														●				'Wareana' — *Thuja occidentalis 'Wareana'*

Plant Functions

	Fragrance (p. 24-26)	Texture (p. 27)	Wind Effects (p. 28)	Climbing & Swinging (p. 30)	Hiding Places (p. 31-32)	Play Props (p. 33-36)	Fruits, Herbs & Nuts (p. 38-39)	Fall Color (p. 41-42)	Winter Berries & Evgrns. (p. 43-46)	Winter Tracery & Bark (p. 47-48)	Winter Flowers (p. 49)	Spring Harbingers (p. 50-51)	Shade Quality (p. 53)	Physical Barriers (p. 55)	Wind Screens/Visual Buffers (p. 56)	Wildlife Enhancement (p. 58-59)	Erosion Control (p. 61)	Drought Tolerance (p. 63-66)
Ash																		
Green *Fraxinus pennsylvanica*										●								●
White *Fraxinus americana*								●		●								●
Aucuba, Japanese *Aucuba japonica*									●									
Azalea ᴴᵀ *Rhododendron spp.*												●						
Balm																		
Bee *Monarda didyma*	●																	
Lemmon *Melissa offcinalis*							●											
Bamboo																		
Heavenly *Nandina domestica*						●		●	●									
Blue Clump *Semiarundinaria spp.*					●													
Golden-groove *Phyllostachys aureosulcata*					●													
Hedge *Bambusa glaucescens*					●													

Plant Functions

	Fragrance (p. 24-26)	Texture (p. 27)	Wind Effects (p. 28)	Climbing & Swinging (p. 30)	Hiding Places (p. 31-32)	Play Props (p. 33-36)	Fruits, Herbs & Nuts (p. 38-39)	Fall Color (p. 41-42)	Winter Berries & Evgrns. (p. 43-46)	Winter Tracery & Bark (p. 47-48)	Winter Flowers (p. 49)	Spring Harbingers (p. 50-51)	Shade Quality (p. 53)	Physical Barriers (p. 55)	Wind Screens/Visual Buffers (p. 56)	Wildlife Enhancement (p. 58-59)	Erosion Control (p. 61)	Drought Tolerance (p. 63-66)
Barberry																		
Japanese *Berberis thunbergii*									●					●				
Korean *Berberis koreana*									●					●				
Mentor *Berberis* x *mentorensis*														●				
Paleleaf *Berberis candidula*									●					●				
Wintergreen *Berberis julianae*														●				
Bayberry *Myrica pensylvanica*	●					●			●								●	●
Beautyberry																		
Japanese *Callicarpa japonica*					●													
Purple *Callicarpa dichotoma*						●												
Beech, American *Fagus grandifolia*				●														
Birch																		
Cutleaf European White *Betula pendula 'Gracilis'*					●													

Plant Functions

	Fragrance (p. 24-26)	Texture (p. 27)	Wind Effects (p. 28)	Climbing & Swinging (p. 30)	Hiding Places (p. 31-32)	Play Props (p. 33-36)	Fruits, Herbs & Nuts (p. 38-39)	Fall Color (p. 41-42)	Winter Berries & Evgrns. (p. 43-46)	Winter Tracery & Bark (p. 47-48)	Winter Flowers (p. 49)	Spring Harbingers (p. 50-51)	Shade Quality (p. 53)	Physical Barriers (p. 55)	Wind Screens/Visual Buffers (p. 56)	Wildlife Enhancement (p. 58-59)	Erosion Control (p. 61)	Drought Tolerance (p. 63-66)
Birch (contd.)																		
Gray																●		●
Betula populifolia																		
Paper (White)										●						●		
Betula papyrifera																		
River			●							●						●		●
Betula nigra																		
Sweet			●					●					●			●		●
Betula lenta																		
Blueberry																		
Highbush							●									●		●
Vaccinium corymbosum																		
Lowbush							●									●		●
Vaccinium angustifolium																		
Bottlebrush, Weeping					●													
Callistemon viminalis 'Red Cascade'																		
Buffalo berry																		●
Shepherdia canadensis																		
Butterfly bush	●															●		
Buddleia davidii																		
Camellia, Common											●							
Camellia japonica																		

Plants for Play

Plant Functions

Plant	Fragrance (p. 24-26)	Texture (p. 27)	Wind Effects (p. 28)	Climbing & Swinging (p. 30)	Hiding Places (p. 31-32)	Play Props (p. 33-36)	Fruits, Herbs & Nuts (p. 38-39)	Fall Color (p. 41-42)	Winter Berries & Evrgrns. (p. 43-46)	Winter Tracery & Bark (p. 47-48)	Winter Flowers (p. 49)	Spring Harbingers (p. 50-51)	Shade Quality (p. 53)	Physical Barriers (p. 55)	Wind Screens/Visual Buffers (p. 56)	Wildlife Enhancement (p. 58-59)	Erosion Control (p. 61)	Drought Tolerance (p. 63-66)
Ceanothus *Ceanothus spp.*																		●
Cedar, Eastern Red *Juniperus virginiana*	●								●						●	●		●
Chamomile *Chamaemelum nobile*	●						●											
Chaste tree *Vitex agnus-castus*	●																	
Cherry Cornelian *Cornus mas*											●							
Pin *Prunus pensylvanica*							●											
Chestnut, Chinese *Castenea mollissima*							●											
Chive *Allium schoenoprasum*							●											
Chokeberry, Red *Aronica arbutifolia*									●									
Chokecherry, Common *Prunus virginiana*							●											

Plant Functions

	Fragrance (p. 24-26)	Texture (p. 27)	Wind Effects (p. 28)	Climbing & Swinging (p. 30)	Hiding Places (p. 31-32)	Play Props (p. 33-36)	Fruits, Herbs & Nuts (p. 38-39)	Fall Color (p. 41-42)	Winter Berries & Evgrns. (p. 43-46)	Winter Tracery & Bark (p. 47-48)	Winter Flowers (p. 49)	Spring Harbingers (p. 50-51)	Shade Quality (p. 53)	Physical Barriers (p. 55)	Wind Screens/Visual Buffers (p. 56)	Wildlife Enhancement (p. 58-59)	Erosion Control (p. 61)	Drought Tolerance (p. 63-66)
Cinquefoil, Shrubby *Potentilla fruticosa*																		●
Cotoneaster MT *Cotoneaster 'Autumn Fire'*									●									
Cotton, Lavender *Santolina chamaecyparissus*	●								●									
Cranberry, American *Vaccinium macrocarpon*							●											
Cranberry bush, European *Viburnum opulus*					●	●			●									
Currant, Buffalo *Ribes odoratum*							●											
Cypress Leyland *x Cupressocyparis leylandii*		●							●						●			
Cypress Common Bald *Taxodium distichum*			●			●												
Daylily *Hemerocallis spp.*	●																	
Dogwood Chinese *Cornus kousa*								●	●	●			●					

Plant Functions

	Fragrance (p. 24-26)	Texture (p. 27)	Wind Effects (p. 28)	Climbing & Swinging (p. 30)	Hiding Places (p. 31-32)	Play Props (p. 33-36)	Fruits, Herbs & Nuts (p. 38-39)	Fall Color (p. 41-42)	Winter Berries & Evrgrns. (p. 43-46)	Winter Tracery & Bark (p. 47-48)	Winter Flowers (p. 49)	Spring Harbingers (p. 50-51)	Shade Quality (p. 53)	Physical Barriers (p. 55)	Wind Screens/Visual Buffers (p. 56)	Wildlife Enhancement (p. 58-59)	Erosion Control (p. 61)	Drought Tolerance (p. 63-66)
Dogwood (contd.)																		
Flowering								●	●	●			●			●		●
Cornus florida																		
Tartarian																	●	
Cornus alba																		
Elaeagnus, Thorny														●				
Elaeagnus pungens																		
Elderberry, American							●											
Sambucus canadensis																		
Elder, Box																		●
Acer negundo																		
Elm, Chinese				●									●					
Ulmus parvifolia																		
Fern, Sweet	●																●	
Comptonia peregrina																		
Fetterbush						●			●			●						
Pieris floribunda																		
Filbert, European							●											
Corylus avellana																		
Fir																		
Balsam						●			●							●		
Abies balsamea																		

Plant Functions

	Fragrance (p. 24-26)	Texture (p. 27)	Wind Effects (p. 28)	Climbing & Swinging (p. 30)	Hiding Places (p. 31-32)	Play Props (p. 33-36)	Fruits, Herbs & Nuts (p. 38-39)	Fall Color (p. 41-42)	Winter Berries & Evrgrns. (p. 43-46)	Winter Tracery & Bark (p. 47-48)	Winter Flowers (p. 49)	Spring Harbingers (p. 50-51)	Shade Quality (p. 53)	Physical Barriers (p. 55)	Wind Screens/Visual Buffers (p. 56)	Wildlife Enhancement (p. 58-59)	Erosion Control (p. 61)	Drought Tolerance (p. 63-66)
Fir (contd.)																		
Fraser						●			●									
Abies fraseri																		
Veitch						●			●									
Abies veitchii																		
White									●							●		
Abies concolor																		
Fire thorn, Scarlet									●					●				
Pyracantha coccinea																		
Fothergilla																		
Dwarf	●							●			●	●						●
Fothergilla gardenii																		
Large	●							●										●
Fothergilla major																		
Forsythia																		
Border																	●	
Forsythia x intermedia																		
Weeping																	●	
Forsythia suspensa																		
Fringe tree	●				●					●						●		
Chionanthus virginicus																		

Plant Functions

	Fragrance (p. 24-26)	Texture (p. 27)	Wind Effects (p. 28)	Climbing & Swinging (p. 30)	Hiding Places (p. 31-32)	Play Props (p. 33-36)	Fruits, Herbs & Nuts (p. 38-39)	Fall Color (p. 41-42)	Winter Berries & Evgrns. (p. 43-46)	Winter Tracery & Bark (p. 47-48)	Winter Flowers (p. 49)	Spring Harbingers (p. 50-51)	Shade Quality (p. 53)	Physical Barriers (p. 55)	Wind Screens/Visual Buffers (p. 56)	Wildlife Enhancement (p. 58-59)	Erosion Control (p. 61)	Drought Tolerance (p. 63-66)
Geranium *Pelargonium spp.*							●											
Geranium, Bigroot *Geranium macrorrhizum*	●																	
Germander, Chamaedrys *Teucrium chamaedrys*	●								●									
Glory-of-the-snow *Chionodoxa luciliae*												●						
Golden-bells *Forsythia x intermedia*												●						
Golden-rain tree *Koelreuteria paniculata*			●															●
Gum, American Sweet *Liquidambar styraciflua*								●										
Gum tree *Eucalyptus spp.*															●			
Grass Feather Reed *Calamagrostis acutiflora 'Stricta'*						●												
Fountain *Pennisetum setaceum*		●	●			●												
Giant Feather *Stipa gigantea*					●													

Plant Functions

	Fragrance (p. 24-26)	Texture (p. 27)	Wind Effects (p. 28)	Climbing & Swinging (p. 30)	Hiding Places (p. 31-32)	Play Props (p. 33-36)	Fruits, Herbs & Nuts (p. 38-39)	Fall Color (p. 41-42)	Winter Berries & Evergrns. (p. 43-46)	Winter Tracery & Bark (p. 47-48)	Winter Flowers (p. 49)	Spring Harbingers (p. 50-51)	Shade Quality (p. 53)	Physical Barriers (p. 55)	Wind Screens/Visual Buffers (p. 56)	Wildlife Enhancement (p. 58-59)	Erosion Control (p. 61)	Drought Tolerance (p. 63-66)
Grass (contd.)																		
Prairie Cord					●													
Spartina pectinata																		
Ravena					●													
Erianthus ravennae																		
Reed						●												
Calamagrostis arundinaceae																		
Silver					●													
Miscanthus spp.																		
Switch					●													
Panicum virgatum																		
Hackberry, Common				●														●
Celtis occidentalis																		
Hawthorn, Yeddo	●								●									
Raphiolepis umbellata																		
Hazelnut, Western							●											
Corylus californica																		
Hazel																		
Common Witch						●												
Hamamelis virginiana																		
Chinese Witch	●											●						
Hamamelis mollis																		

Plants for Play

Plant Functions

	Fragrance (p. 24-26)	Texture (p. 27)	Wind Effects (p. 28)	Climbing & Swinging (p. 30)	Hiding Places (p. 31-32)	Play Props (p. 33-36)	Fruits, Herbs & Nuts (p. 38-39)	Fall Color (p. 41-42)	Winter Berries & Evrgrns. (p. 43-46)	Winter Tracery & Bark (p. 47-48)	Winter Flowers (p. 49)	Spring Harbingers (p. 50-51)	Shade Quality (p. 53)	Physical Barriers (p. 55)	Wind Screens/Visual Buffers (p. 56)	Wildlife Enhancement (p. 58-59)	Erosion Control (p. 61)	Drought Tolerance (p. 63-66)
Hazel (contd.)																		
Vernal Witch						●					●							
Hamamelis vernalis																		
Hemlock																		
Canada						●			●						●	●		
Tsuga canadensis																		
Carolina						●			●						●			
Tsuga caroliniana																		
Honeysuckle																		
Common	●																	
Lonicera periclymenum																		
Etruscan	●																	
Lonicera etrusca 'Superba'																		
Gold Flame	●																	
Lonicera x heckrottii																		
Privet	●																	
Lonicer apilenta																		
Sweet	●																	
Lonicera caprifolium																		
Winter	●																	
Lonicera fragrantissima																		

Plant Functions

	Fragrance (p. 24-26)	Texture (p. 27)	Wind Effects (p. 28)	Climbing & Swinging (p. 30)	Hiding Places (p. 31-32)	Play Props (p. 33-36)	Fruits, Herbs & Nuts (p. 38-39)	Fall Color (p. 41-42)	Winter Berries & Evrgrns. (p. 43-46)	Winter Tracery & Bark (p. 47-48)	Winter Flowers (p. 49)	Spring Harbingers (p. 50-51)	Shade Quality (p. 53)	Physical Barriers (p. 55)	Wind Screens/Visual Buffers (p. 56)	Wildlife Enhancement (p. 58-59)	Erosion Control (p. 61)	Drought Tolerance (p. 63-66)
Hornbeam																		
American																		●
Carpinus caroliniana																		
European																		●
Carpinus betulus																		
Hyacinth, Grape																		
Muscari armeniacum												●						
Jasmine																		
Confederate	●																	
Trachelospermum jasminoides																		
Poet's	●																	
Jasminum officinale																		
Yellow Star	●																	
Trachelospermum asiaticum																		
Winter											●						●	
Jasminum nudiflorum																		
Juniper																		
Hetz Blue	●								●									●
Juniperus chinensis 'Hetzii'																		
Pfitzer	●								●									●
Juniperus chinensis 'Pfitzerana'																		
Sargent	●								●								●	●
Juniperus chinensis var. sargentii																		

Plants for Play

Plant Functions

Fragrance (p. 24-26)	Texture (p. 27)	Wind Effects (p. 28)	Climbing & Swinging (p. 30)	Hiding Places (p. 31-32)	Play Props (p. 33-36)	Fruits, Herbs & Nuts (p. 38-39)	Fall Color (p. 41-42)	Winter Berries & Evgrns. (p. 43-46)	Winter Tracery & Bark (p. 47-48)	Winter Flowers (p. 49)	Spring Harbingers (p. 50-51)	Shade Quality (p. 53)	Physical Barriers (p. 55)	Wind Screens/Visual Buffers (p. 56)	Wildlife Enhancement (p. 58-59)	Erosion Control (p. 61)	Drought Tolerance (p. 63-66)	
									●									**Katsura tree** *Cercidiphyllum japonicum*
	●					●												**Kiwi Fruit** *Actinidia chinensis*
	●				●													**Lamb's Ears** *Stachys byzantina*
●						●												**Lavender, English** *Lavandula angustifolia*
																	●	**Lilac** Common *Syringa vulgaris*
																	●	Persian *Syringa persica*
●																		**Lily, Fragrant plantain** *Hosta plantaginea*
								●			●							**Lily-of-the-valley bush** *Pieris japonica*
								●										**Lilyturf** Big Blue *Liriope muscari*
								●										Creeping *Liriope spicata*

Plant Functions

	Fragrance (p. 24-26)	Texture (p. 27)	Wind Effects (p. 28)	Climbing & Swinging (p. 30)	Hiding Places (p. 31-32)	Play Props (p. 33-36)	Fruits, Herbs & Nuts (p. 38-39)	Fall Color (p. 41-42)	Winter Berries & Evrgrns. (p. 43-46)	Winter Tracery & Bark (p. 47-48)	Winter Flowers (p. 49)	Spring Harbingers (p. 50-51)	Shade Quality (p. 53)	Physical Barriers (p. 55)	Wind Screens/Visual Buffers (p. 56)	Wildlife Enhancement (p. 58-59)	Erosion Control (p. 61)	Drought Tolerance (p. 63-66)
Linden, Small-leaved *Tilia cordata*													●					
Locust Black [MT] *Robinia pseudoacacia*																		●
Idaho *Robinia ambigua 'Idahoensis'*																		●
Thornless Honey *Gleditsia triacanthos* var. *inermis*			●					●		●			●					●
Magnolia Saucer *Magnolia x soulangiana*						●				●		●						
Southern *Magnolia grandiflora*	●				●	●			●									
Star *Magnolia stellata*	●					●						●						
Sweet bay *Magnolia virginiana*	●					●			●									
Maidenhair tree *Ginkgo biloba*								●										●
Maple Amur *Acer ginnala*					●	●		●		●								

Plant Functions

Fragrance (p. 24-26)	Texture (p. 27)	Wind Effects (p. 28)	Climbing & Swinging (p. 30)	Hiding Places (p. 31-32)	Play Props (p. 33-36)	Fruits, Herbs & Nuts (p. 38-39)	Fall Color (p. 41-42)	Winter Berries & Evgrns. (p. 43-46)	Winter Tracery & Bark (p. 47-48)	Winter Flowers (p. 49)	Spring Harbingers (p. 50-51)	Shade Quality (p. 53)	Physical Barriers (p. 55)	Wind Screens/Visual Buffers (p. 56)	Wildlife Enhancement (p. 58-59)	Erosion Control (p. 61)	Drought Tolerance (p. 63-66)	
																		Maple (contd.)
				●	●		●										●	Hedge
																		Acer campestre
		●		●	●		●		●									Japanese
																		Acer palmatum
					●		●		●									Nikko
																		Acer maximowiczianum
																	●	Norway
																		Acer platanoides
									●									Paperbark
																		Acer griseum
		●	●				●					●			●		●	Red
																		Acer rubrum
			●				●		●			●			●			Sugar
																		Acer saccharum
																	●	Trident
																		Acer buergerianum
																		Mimosa
											●							Golden
																		Acacia baileyana
												●						Silk tree
																		Albizia julibrissin

Plant Functions

	Fragrance (p. 24-26)	Texture (p. 27)	Wind Effects (p. 28)	Climbing & Swinging (p. 30)	Hiding Places (p. 31-32)	Play Props (p. 33-36)	Fruits, Herbs & Nuts (p. 38-39)	Fall Color (p. 41-42)	Winter Berries & Evrgrns. (p. 43-46)	Winter Tracery & Bark (p. 47-48)	Winter Flowers (p. 49)	Spring Harbingers (p. 50-51)	Shade Quality (p. 53)	Physical Barriers (p. 55)	Wind Screens/Visual Buffers (p. 56)	Wildlife Enhancement (p. 58-59)	Erosion Control (p. 61)	Drought Tolerance (p. 63-66)
Mint, Pineapple																		
Mentha suaveolens 'Variegata'							●											
Money plant																		
Lunaria annua			●			●												
Lunaria annua 'Variegata'			●			●												
Mulberry																		
Paper																		
Broussonetia papyrifera																		●
Red																		
Morus rubra							●											
Myrtle																		
Crape																		
Lagerstroemia indica			●							●								
Pacific Wax																		
Myrica californica									●									
Wax																		
Myrica cerifera	●					●			●								●	
Nasturtium																		
Canary Creeper																		
Tropaeolum peregrinum							●											
Garden																		
Tropaeolum majus							●											

Plants for Play

Plant Functions

Fragrance (p. 24-26)	Texture (p. 27)	Wind Effects (p. 28)	Climbing & Swinging (p. 30)	Hiding Places (p. 31-32)	Play Props (p. 33-36)	Fruits, Herbs & Nuts (p. 38-39)	Fall Color (p. 41-42)	Winter Berries & Evgrns. (p. 43-46)	Winter Tracery & Bark (p. 47-48)	Winter Flowers (p. 49)	Spring Harbingers (p. 50-51)	Shade Quality (p. 53)	Physical Barriers (p. 55)	Wind Screens/Visual Buffers (p. 56)	Wildlife Enhancement (p. 58-59)	Erosion Control (p. 61)	Drought Tolerance (p. 63-66)	
																		Nasturtium (contd.)
						●												Wreath
																		Tropaeolum polyphyllum
																		Oak
								●										Chinese Evergreen
																		Quercus myrsinifolia
														●				Laurel
																		Quercus imbricaria
									●									Pin
																		Quercus palustris
					●		●		●									Red
																		Quercus rubra
			●									●						Sawtooth
																		Quercus acutissima
					●													Water
																		Quercus nigra
			●		●				●			●			●			White
																		Quercus alba
			●		●							●						Willow
																		Quercus phellos
												●						**Olive**
																		Olea europaea

Plant Functions

	Fragrance (p. 24-26)	Texture (p. 27)	Wind Effects (p. 28)	Climbing & Swinging (p. 30)	Hiding Places (p. 31-32)	Play Props (p. 33-36)	Fruits, Herbs & Nuts (p. 38-39)	Fall Color (p. 41-42)	Winter Berries & Evrgrns. (p. 43-46)	Winter Tracery & Bark (p. 47-48)	Winter Flowers (p. 49)	Spring Harbingers (p. 50-51)	Shade Quality (p. 53)	Physical Barriers (p. 55)	Wind Screens/Visual Buffers (p. 56)	Wildlife Enhancement (p. 58-59)	Erosion Control (p. 61)	Drought Tolerance (p. 63-66)
Olive, Russian *Elaeagnus angustifolia*	●		●															●
Oregano *Origanum vulgare*							●											
Pagoda tree, Japanese *Sophora japonica*				●						●			●					
Sophora japonica 'Regent'																		●
Pecan *Carya illinoinensis*						●	●						●			●		●
Peppermint *Mentha x piperita*							●											
Periwinkle, Dwarf *Vinca minor*																	●	
Photinia Chinese *Photinia serrulata*									●						●			
Fraser *Photinia x fraseri*					●				●						●			
Japanese *Photinia glabra*					●				●						●			
Persimmon, Common *Diospyros virginiana*							●											

Plant Functions

	Fragrance (p. 24-26)	Texture (p. 27)	Wind Effects (p. 28)	Climbing & Swinging (p. 30)	Hiding Places (p. 31-32)	Play Props (p. 33-36)	Fruits, Herbs & Nuts (p. 38-39)	Fall Color (p. 41-42)	Winter Berries & Evgrns. (p. 43-46)	Winter Tracery & Bark (p. 47-48)	Winter Flowers (p. 49)	Spring Harbingers (p. 50-51)	Shade Quality (p. 53)	Physical Barriers (p. 55)	Wind Screens/Visual Buffers (p. 56)	Wildlife Enhancement (p. 58-59)	Erosion Control (p. 61)	Drought Tolerance (p. 63-66)
Pine																		
Austrian — *Pinus nigra*	●					●			●									
Aleppo — *Pinus halepensis*				●														
Eastern White — *Pinus strobus*	●					●			●						●	●		
Japanese Black — *Pinus thunbergii*				●														
Italian Stone — *Pinus pinea*				●														
Mountain — *Pinus mugo*	●					●			●									
Red — *Pinus resinosa*	●					●			●							●		●
Scotch — *Pinus sylvestris*	●					●			●									
Pink, Cottage — *Dianthus plumarius*	●																	
Pistache, Chinese — *Pistacia chinensis*				●									●					

Plant Functions

	Fragrance (p. 24-26)	Texture (p. 27)	Wind Effects (p. 28)	Climbing & Swinging (p. 30)	Hiding Places (p. 31-32)	Play Props (p. 33-36)	Fruits, Herbs & Nuts (p. 38-39)	Fall Color (p. 41-42)	Winter Berries & Evgrns. (p. 43-46)	Winter Tracery & Bark (p. 47-48)	Winter Flowers (p. 49)	Spring Harbingers (p. 50-51)	Shade Quality (p. 53)	Physical Barriers (p. 55)	Wind Screens/Visual Buffers (p. 56)	Wildlife Enhancement (p. 58-59)	Erosion Control (p. 61)	Drought Tolerance (p. 63-66)
Pittosporum																		
Japanese					●													
Pittosporum tobira																		
Victorian Box					●													
Pittosporum undulatum																		
Plum, American							●											
Prunus americana																		
Pomegranate							●											
Punica granatum																		
Quince																		
Flowering														●				
Chaenomeles speciosa																		
Japanese												●						
Chaenomeles japonica																		
Redbud																		
Eastern						●				●		●						●
Cercis canadensis																		
Western												●						
Cercis occidentalis																		
Redwood, Dawn			●							●								
Metasequoia glyptostroboides																		
Rhododendron HT												●						
Rhododendron spp.																		

Plant Functions

	Fragrance (p. 24-26)	Texture (p. 27)	Wind Effects (p. 28)	Climbing & Swinging (p. 30)	Hiding Places (p. 31-32)	Play Props (p. 33-36)	Fruits, Herbs & Nuts (p. 38-39)	Fall Color (p. 41-42)	Winter Berries & Evergrns. (p. 43-46)	Winter Tracery & Bark (p. 47-48)	Winter Flowers (p. 49)	Spring Harbingers (p. 50-51)	Shade Quality (p. 53)	Physical Barriers (p. 55)	Wind Screens/Visual Buffers (p. 56)	Wildlife Enhancement (p. 58-59)	Erosion Control (p. 61)	Drought Tolerance (p. 63-66)
Rose																		
Carolina — *Rosa carolina*																		●
Rugosa — *Rosa rugosa*	●													●				●
Memorial — *Rosa wichuriana*	●																●	
Rose-of -Sharon — *Hibiscus syriacus*						●												
Rosemary — *Rosmarinus officinalis*							●											
Sage — *Salvia officinalis*							●											
Silverbell, Carolina — *Halesia carolina*						●		●		●			●					
Skimmia																		
Japanese — *Skimmia japonica*						●			●			●						
Reeves — *Skimmia reevesiana*									●			●						
Smoke Tree, American — *Cotinus obovatus*		●			●	●		●										●

Plants for Play

Plant Functions

	Fragrance (p. 24-26)	Texture (p. 27)	Wind Effects (p. 28)	Climbing & Swinging (p. 30)	Hiding Places (p. 31-32)	Play Props (p. 33-36)	Fruits, Herbs & Nuts (p. 38-39)	Fall Color (p. 41-42)	Winter Berries & Evrgrns. (p. 43-46)	Winter Tracery & Bark (p. 47-48)	Winter Flowers (p. 49)	Spring Harbingers (p. 50-51)	Shade Quality (p. 53)	Physical Barriers (p. 55)	Wind Screens/Visual Buffers (p. 56)	Wildlife Enhancement (p. 58-59)	Erosion Control (p. 61)	Drought Tolerance (p. 63-66)
Snowflake, Spring *Leucojum vernum*	●											●						
Sourwood *Oxydendrum arboreum*								●										●
Spearmint *Mentha spicata*							●											
Spicebush *Lindera benzoin*	●							●								●		
Spindle tree, Winged *Euonymus alatus*								●										
Spruce Black *Picea mariana*						●			●							●		●
Narrow Oriental *Picea orientalis*						●			●									
Norway *Picea abies*															●			
Serbian *Picea omorika*															●			
White *Picea glauca*						●			●							●		●
Spurge, Japanese *Pachysandra terminalis*																	●	

Plant Functions

	Fragrance (p. 24-26)	Texture (p. 27)	Wind Effects (p. 28)	Climbing & Swinging (p. 30)	Hiding Places (p. 31-32)	Play Props (p. 33-36)	Fruits, Herbs & Nuts (p. 38-39)	Fall Color (p. 41-42)	Winter Berries & Evrgrns. (p. 43-46)	Winter Tracery & Bark (p. 47-48)	Winter Flowers (p. 49)	Spring Harbingers (p. 50-51)	Shade Quality (p. 53)	Physical Barriers (p. 55)	Wind Screens/Visual Buffers (p. 56)	Wildlife Enhancement (p. 58-59)	Erosion Control (p. 61)	Drought Tolerance (p. 63-66)
Stonecrop *Sedum spp.*		●				●												
Sumac, Fragrant *Rhus aromatica*						●										●	●	
Summer-sweet *Clethra alnifolia*	●							●									●	●
Sycamore, Eastern *Platanus occidentalis*				●		●				●			●					●
Sweet shrub, Common *Calycanthus floridus*	●																	
Thyme Common *Thymus vulgaris*							●											
Lemon *Thymus x citriodorus*	●						●											
Tulip tree, American *Liriodendron tulipifera*								●		●								
Viburnum Arrowwood *Viburnum dentatum*						●		●									●	
Black Haw *Viburnum prunifolium*					●	●		●										●

Plant Functions

	Fragrance (p. 24-26)	Texture (p. 27)	Wind Effects (p. 28)	Climbing & Swinging (p. 30)	Hiding Places (p. 31-32)	Play Props (p. 33-36)	Fruits, Herbs & Nuts (p. 38-39)	Fall Color (p. 41-42)	Winter Berries & Evrgrns. (p. 43-46)	Winter Tracery & Bark (p. 47-48)	Winter Flowers (p. 49)	Spring Harbingers (p. 50-51)	Shade Quality (p. 53)	Physical Barriers (p. 55)	Wind Screens/Visual Buffers (p. 56)	Wildlife Enhancement (p. 58-59)	Erosion Control (p. 61)	Drought Tolerance (p. 63-66)
Viburnum (contd.)																		
Double-file *Viburnum plicatum tomentosum*			●		●	●		●								●		
Judd *Viburnum x juddii*	●																	
Korean Spice *Viburnum carlesii*	●											●						
Linden *Viburnum dilatatum*								●										
Leatherleaf *Viburnum rhytidophyllum*									●						●			
Nannyberry *Viburnum lentago*						●											●	●
Willow																		
Goat *Salix caprea*		●				●						●						
Pussy *Salix discolor*						●												
Weeping *Salix babylonica*					●					●								
Wintercreeper *Euonymus forunei*									●									

Plant Functions

	Fragrance (p. 24-26)	Texture (p. 27)	Wind Effects (p. 28)	Climbing & Swinging (p. 30)	Hiding Places (p. 31-32)	Play Props (p. 33-36)	Fruits, Herbs & Nuts (p. 38-39)	Fall Color (p. 41-42)	Winter Berries & Evrgrns. (p. 43-46)	Winter Tracery & Bark (p. 47-48)	Winter Flowers (p. 49)	Spring Harbingers (p. 50-51)	Shade Quality (p. 53)	Physical Barriers (p. 55)	Wind Screens/Visual Buffers (p. 56)	Wildlife Enhancement (p. 58-59)	Erosion Control (p. 61)	Drought Tolerance (p. 63-66)
Wintergreen *Gaultheria procumbens*	●							●	●									●
Wintersweet, Fragrant *Chimonanthus praecox*	●										●							
Woodruff, Sweet *Galium odoratum*	●																	
Yellowwood *Cladrastis lutea*				●						●			●					
Zelkova, Japanese *Zelkova serrata*				●						●			●					

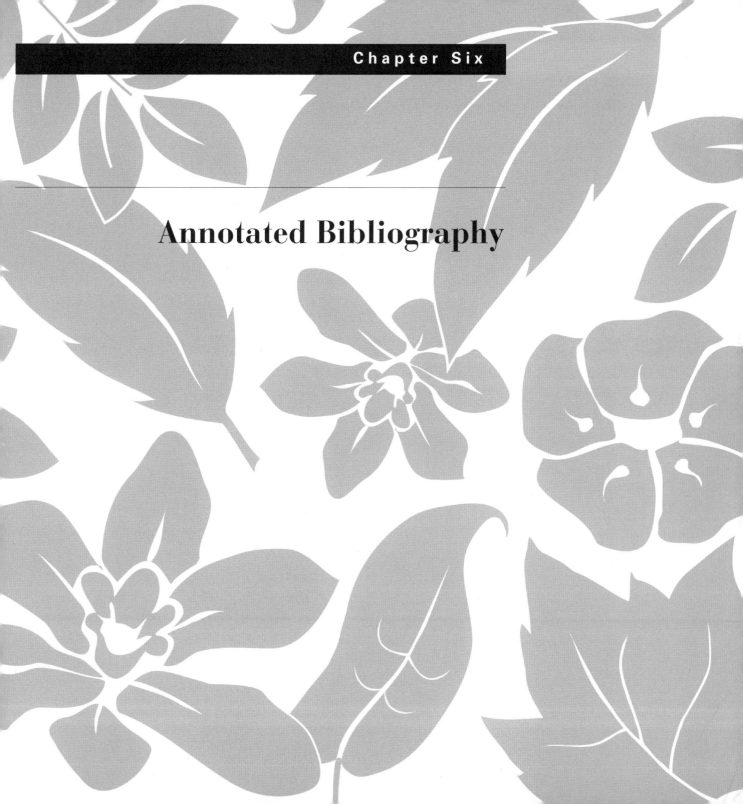

Chapter Six

Annotated Bibliography

Bailey, Liberty H.; and Bailey, Ethel Z.; revised and expanded by the staff of the L.H. Bailey Hortorium, Cornell University. *Hortus Third: A Concise Dictionary of Plants Cultivated in the United States and Canada*. New York: Macmillan Publishing Company, 1976. ISBN 0-02-505470-8

This is widely considered the authoritative reference for plants in the U.S. and Canada. It contains nearly 24,000 entries. Written for advanced horticulturalists and others interested in cultivated plants, it is sparsely illustrated (260 line drawings). But if a plant exists in the U.S. or Canada, your likely to find it here with information on its characteristics and habitat.

Brickell, Christopher, ed. *The American Horticultural Society Encyclopedia of Garden Plants*. New York: Macmillan Publishing Company, 1989. ISBN 0-02-557920-7

This is the American version of the *Royal Horticultural Society Encyclopedia of Garden Plants* (published in London by Dorling Kindersley). Over 8,000 plants are listed in this excellent guide, more than 4,000 of which are illustrated with color photographs in a "plant catalog" that is systematically arranged by plant type, size, season of interest, and color. Every plant description includes information on size, shape, prefered light and soil conditions, and hardiness rating.

Creasy, Rosalind. *Edible Landscaping*. San Francisco: Sierra Club Books, 1982. ISBN 0-87156-249-9; 0-87156-278-2 (pbk.)

A broad treatment of how to design food-bearing, tastable landscapes. Although the focus is on backyards, the book is an excellent source of information that can be applied in other gardening and landscape contexts.

Dirr, Michael A. *Manual of Woody Landscape Plants: Their Identification, Ornamental Characteristics, Culture, Propagation and Uses.* 3rd edition. Champaign, IL: Stipes Publishing Co., 1983. ISBN 0-87563-344-7

Over 1000 species are listed and many cultivars are cited. Each listing includes detailed information on: Leaves, Buds, Stem, Size, Hardiness, Habit, Rate, Texture, Bark, Leaf Color, Flowers, Fruit, Culture, Diseases & Insects, Landscape Value, Propagation, and Additional Notes. Illustrated with line drawings.

Halfacre, R. Gordon; and Shawcroft, Anne R. *Landscape Plants of the Southeast.* 5th ed. Raleigh, NC: Sparks Press, 1989. ISBN 0-916822-14-1

This is a useful reference for designers in the Southeast. Organized by plant size, it provides one page of information per plant, including color photos and just about the right amount of detail. Not fully comprehensive, but an excellent place to start.

Hériteau, Jacqueline. *The National Arboretum Book of Outstanding Garden Plants.* New York: Simon and Schuster, 1990. ISBN 0-671-66957-5

This was the first book published after the USDA issued the new Hardiness Zone Map in January 1990. It provides a comprehensive selection of "1700 proven performers" (i.e., "the most beautiful, durable, and adaptable... that will thrive with the least amount of fertilizing and watering, and that are the most resistant to pests and diseases."). The book is organized by categories that designers will find easy to work with: flowers, aquatic plants, herbs (sure winners with children), ornamental grasses (magnificent, and very appropriate for children's areas), ground covers, vines, shrubs, and trees. There are lengthy narrative descriptions of each plant, but many are not illustrated with photographs.

Hightshoe, Gary L. *Native Trees, Shrubs, and Vines for Urban and Rural America*. New York: Van Nostrand Reinhold, 1988. ISBN 0-442-2327-8

An invaluable source with extensive elimination keys. Over 750 species are included. There are excellent tables on foilage, bud and fruit color, bark characteristics, flower fragrance, and wildlife value. A phenlogical calendar shows flowering, foliage, and fruiting time by month in bar chart.. Plants are listed by botanical name, indexed by common name. Each listing includes information on: form, branching, foliage, flower, fruit, habitat, soil, hardiness, susceptibility, urban tolerance,and associate species. Illustrated with line drawings, maps, and b/w photos.

Lampe, Kenneth F. *AMA Handbook of Poisonous and Injurious Plants*. Chicago: American Medical Association, 1985. ISBN 0-89970-183-3

This book has just about everything you could possibly want to know about poisonous and injurious plants in general and the details of each toxic species in particular, including a photograph of each. It also includes detailed medical descriptions of symptoms and treatments.

Sunset Western Garden Book. Menlo Park, CA: Lane Publishing Co., 1988. ISBN 0-376-03853-5

The book for gardeners in the western U.S. Organized alphabetically by scientific and common names (cross-referenced to the scientific) and containing 1200 line illustrations, the book provides a comprehensive encyclopedia of western plants. An extensive introduction includes discussions of plant care issues and lists of plants that are drought tolerant and deerproof, among others. Plants are zoned by 24 western climate zones.

Tampion, John. *Dangerous Plants*. New York: Universe Books, 1982. ISBN 0-87663-280-0; 0-87663-568-0 (pbk.)

Appendix 1 provides a compilation of poisonous plants. It includes numerous references and differentiates the levels and types of toxicity and dermatitis.

Tull, Delena. *A Practical Guide to Edible and Useful Plants*. Houston, TX: Pacesetter Press, 1987. ISBN 0-87719-022-4

Although poisons are not the main focus, this book is a useful and reasonable guide to poisonous and harmful plants. In Chapter Four, the book differentiates between toxic wild plants and toxic ornamentals; between toxicity and rashes and sneezes. Other chapters discuss more positive aspects of plants, such as teas, spices, and fibers. The book includes an index and is illustrated with line drawings and color photos.

Wyman, Donald. *Shrubs and Vines for American Gardens*. Revised and Enlarged Edition. New York: Macmillan Publishing Co., 1969. ISBN 0-02632160-2

This book lists over 1500 plant species, including many cultivars. It provides a number of lists organized by plant function: Hardiness, Order of Bloom, Ornamental Fruits, Foliage Colors, and Shrubs for Various Purposes. Wyman's expertise lies with plants for the western U.S.

For Additional Information On Plants That Attract Wildlife

There are several useful resource materials that readers may wish to consult for additional information regarding plants that attract wildlife to children's play areas:

Calloway Gardens. *Butterfly Gardening*. Pine Mountain, GA: Calloway Gardens Education Department, n.d.

A free pamphlet available by writing to Calloway Gardens, Education Department, Pine Mountain, GA 31822-2000; tel. (706) 663-5133.

Cawdell, Peter. *Starting a Butterfly Garden*. Lincolnshire, U.K.: School Garden Company, 1987. ISBN 1-85116-801-X

Available by writing to the School Garden Company, P.O. Box 49, Spalding, Lincolnshire, PE11 1NZ, U.K; tel. 0775-69518.

Creasy, Rosalind. *Earthly Delights*. San Francisco: Sierra Club Books, 1985. ISBN 0-87156-841-1; 0-87156-840-3 (pbk)

Contains a chapter titled "The Wildlife Garden" on pp. 89-97.

Matthews, Nigel. *Garden For Birds*. Lincolnshire, U.K.: School Garden Company, 1992. ISBN 1-85116-805-2

Available by writing to the School Garden Company, P.O. Box 49, Spalding, Lincolnshire, PE11 1NZ, U.K; tel. 0775-69518.

National Wildlife Federation. *Planting an Oasis for Wildlife*. Washington, DC: National Wildlife Federation, 1986. ISBN 0-945051-52-2